# BATTLE BEASTS

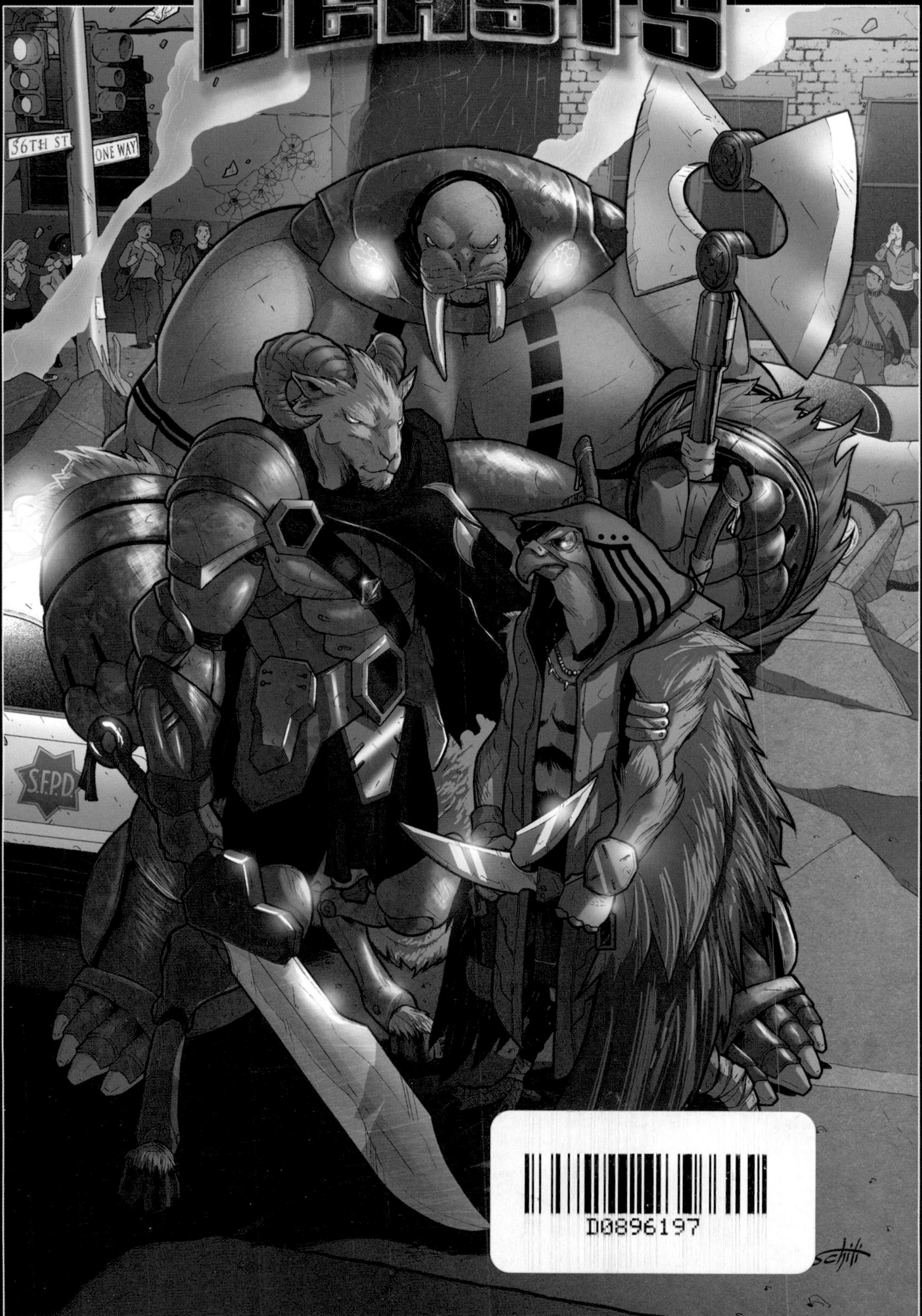
56TH ST
ONE WAY
S.F.P.D.

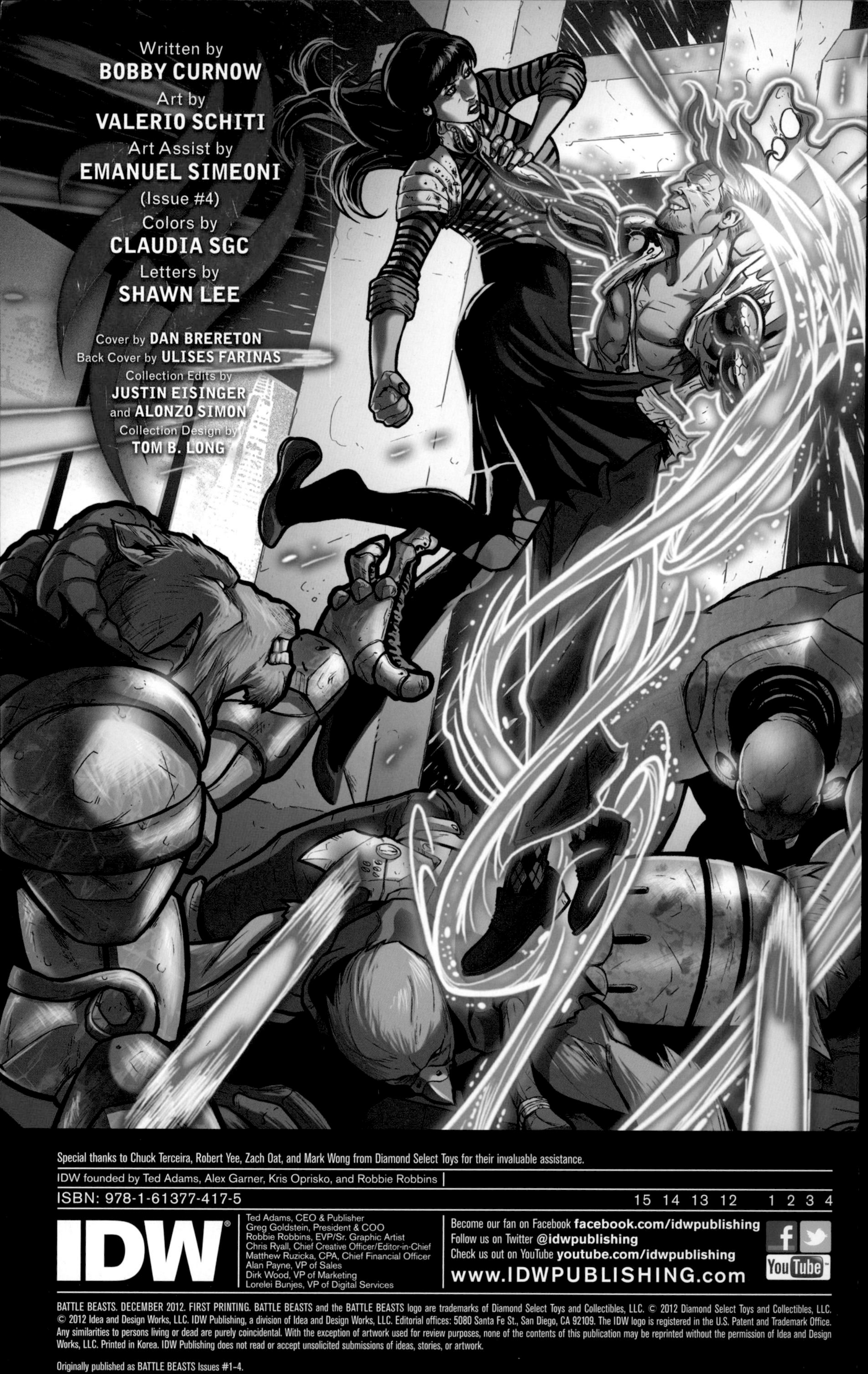
Written by
BOBBY CURNOW
Art by
VALERIO SCHITI
Art Assist by
EMANUEL SIMEONI
(Issue #4)
Colors by
CLAUDIA SGC
Letters by
SHAWN LEE
Cover by DAN BRERETON
Back Cover by ULISES FARINAS
Collection Edits by
JUSTIN EISINGER
and ALONZO SIMON
Collection Design by
TOM B. LONG

Special thanks to Chuck Terceira, Robert Yee, Zach Oat, and Mark Wong from Diamond Select Toys for their invaluable assistance.

IDW founded by Ted Adams, Alex Garner, Kris Oprisko, and Robbie Robbins

ISBN: 978-1-61377-417-5

15 14 13 12 1 2 3 4

Ted Adams, CEO & Publisher
Greg Goldstein, President & COO
Robbie Robbins, EVP/Sr. Graphic Artist
Chris Ryall, Chief Creative Officer/Editor-in-Chief
Matthew Ruzicka, CPA, Chief Financial Officer
Alan Payne, VP of Sales
Dirk Wood, VP of Marketing
Lorelei Bunjes, VP of Digital Services





Originally published as BATTLE BEASTS Issues #1–4.

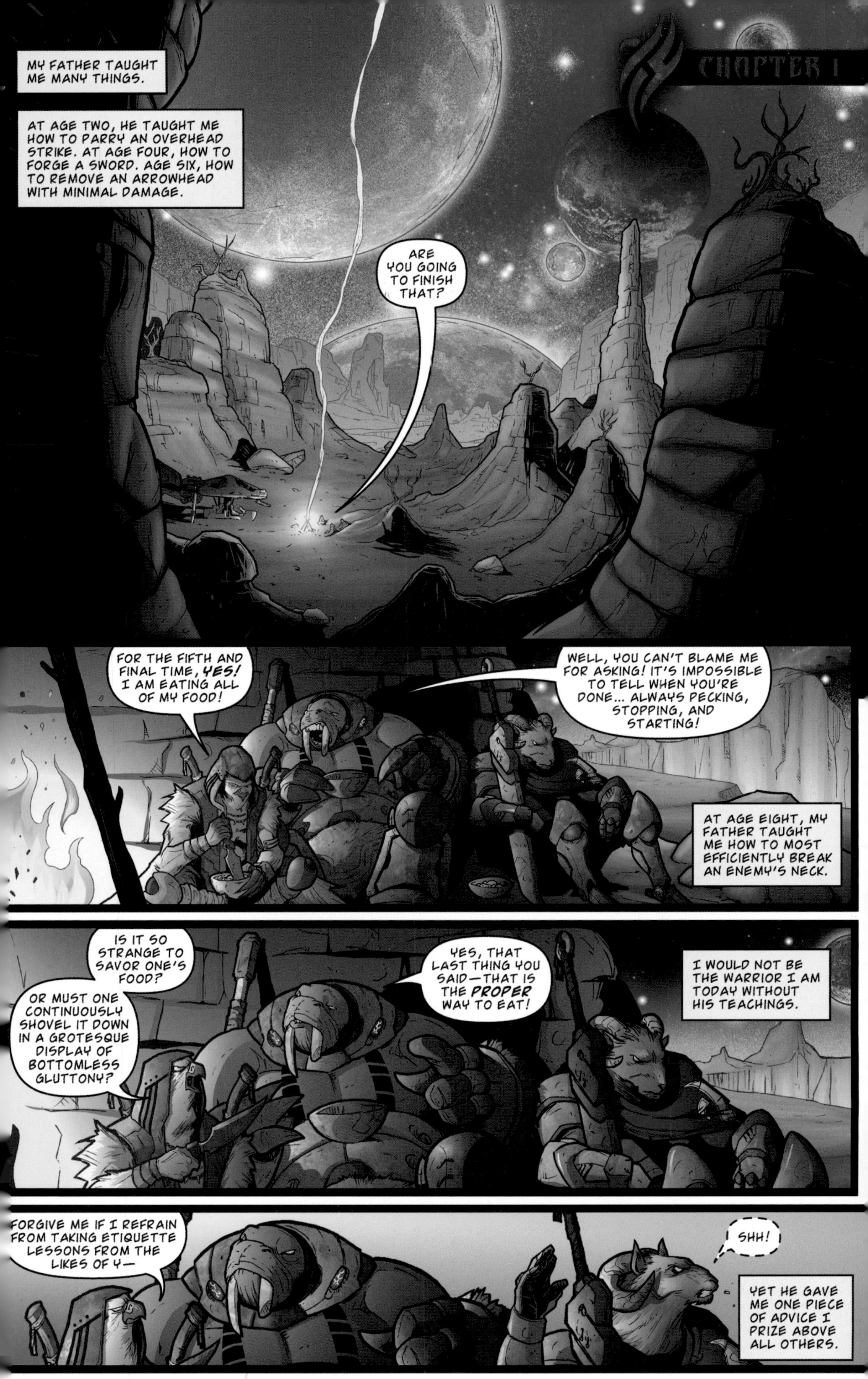

CHAPTER 1
MY FATHER TAUGHT ME MANY THINGS.
AT AGE TWO, HE TAUGHT ME HOW TO PARRY AN OVERHEAD STRIKE. AT AGE FOUR, HOW TO FORGE A SWORD. AGE SIX, HOW TO REMOVE AN ARROWHEAD WITH MINIMAL DAMAGE.
ARE YOU GOING TO FINISH THAT?
FOR THE FIFTH AND FINAL TIME, YES! I AM EATING ALL OF MY FOOD!
WELL, YOU CAN'T BLAME ME FOR ASKING! IT'S IMPOSSIBLE TO TELL WHEN YOU'RE DONE... ALWAYS PECKING, STOPPING, AND STARTING!
AT AGE EIGHT, MY FATHER TAUGHT ME HOW TO MOST EFFICIENTLY BREAK AN ENEMY'S NECK.
IS IT SO STRANGE TO SAVOR ONE'S FOOD?
OR MUST ONE CONTINUOUSLY SHOVEL IT DOWN IN A GROTESQUE DISPLAY OF BOTTOMLESS GLUTTONY?
YES, THAT LAST THING YOU SAID—THAT IS THE PROPER WAY TO EAT!
I WOULD NOT BE THE WARRIOR I AM TODAY WITHOUT HIS TEACHINGS.
FORGIVE ME IF I REFRAIN FROM TAKING ETIQUETTE LESSONS FROM THE LIKES OF Y—
SHH!
YET HE GAVE ME ONE PIECE OF ADVICE I PRIZE ABOVE ALL OTHERS.

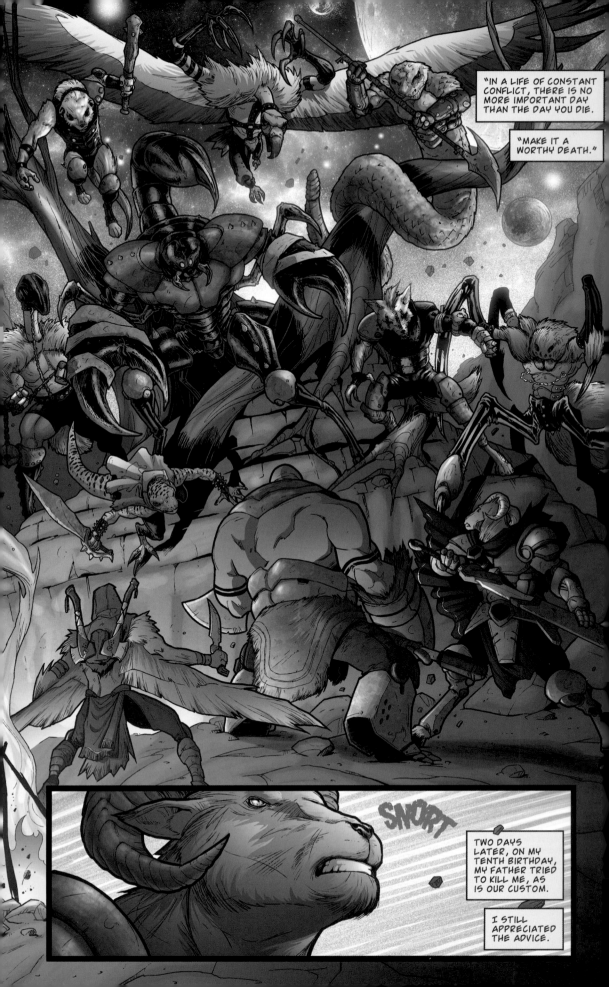

"IN A LIFE OF CONSTANT CONFLICT, THERE IS NO MORE IMPORTANT DAY THAN THE DAY YOU DIE.

"MAKE IT A WORTHY DEATH."

SNORT

TWO DAYS LATER, ON MY TENTH BIRTHDAY, MY FATHER TRIED TO KILL ME, AS IS OUR CUSTOM.

I STILL APPRECIATED THE ADVICE.

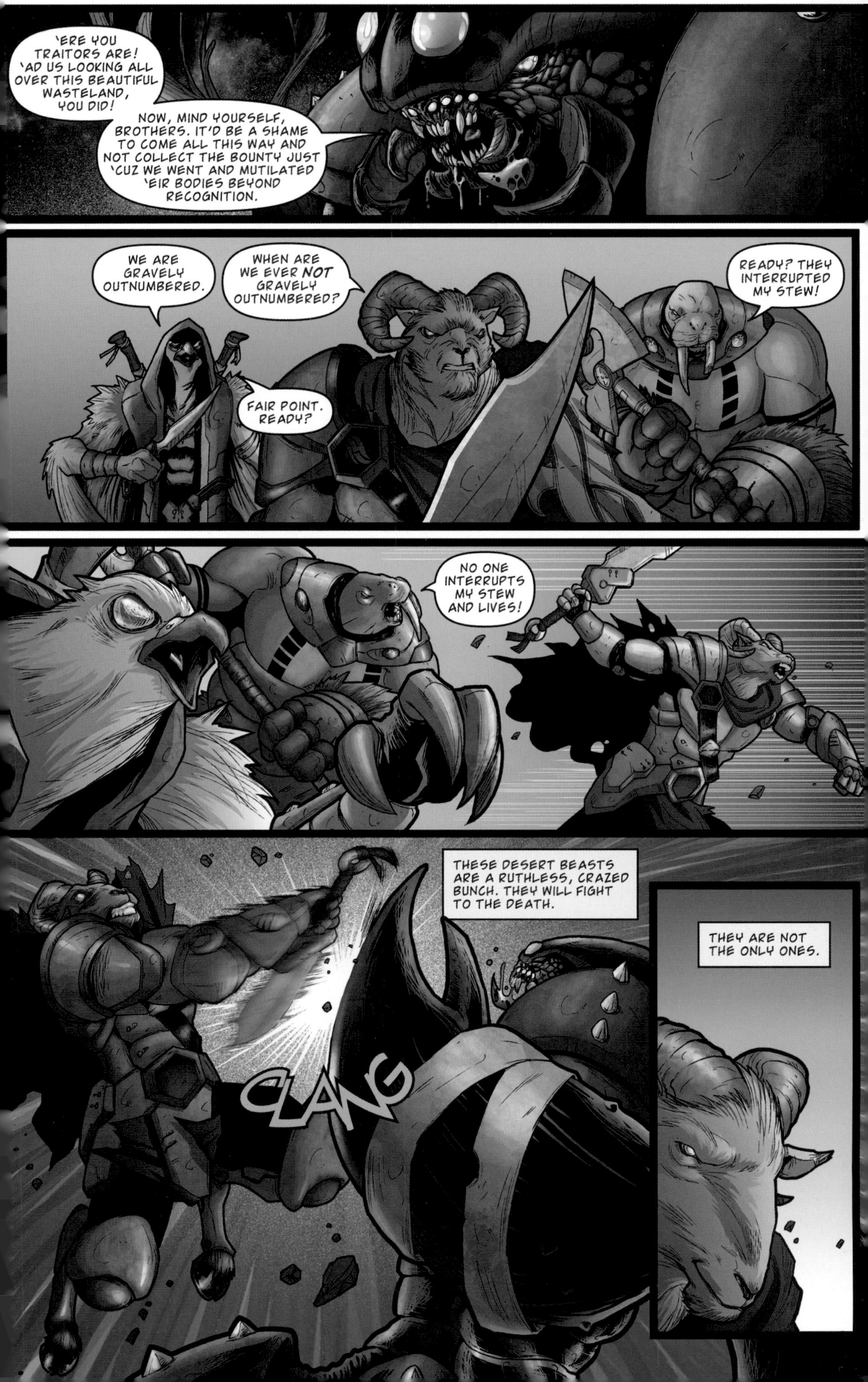
'ERE YOU TRAITORS ARE! 'AD US LOOKING ALL OVER THIS BEAUTIFUL WASTELAND, YOU DID!
NOW, MIND YOURSELF, BROTHERS. IT'D BE A SHAME TO COME ALL THIS WAY AND NOT COLLECT THE BOUNTY JUST 'CUZ WE WENT AND MUTILATED 'EIR BODIES BEYOND RECOGNITION.
WE ARE GRAVELY OUTNUMBERED.
WHEN ARE WE EVER NOT GRAVELY OUTNUMBERED?
FAIR POINT. READY?
READY? THEY INTERRUPTED MY STEW!
NO ONE INTERRUPTS MY STEW AND LIVES!
THESE DESERT BEASTS ARE A RUTHLESS, CRAZED BUNCH. THEY WILL FIGHT TO THE DEATH.
CLANG
THEY ARE NOT THE ONLY ONES.

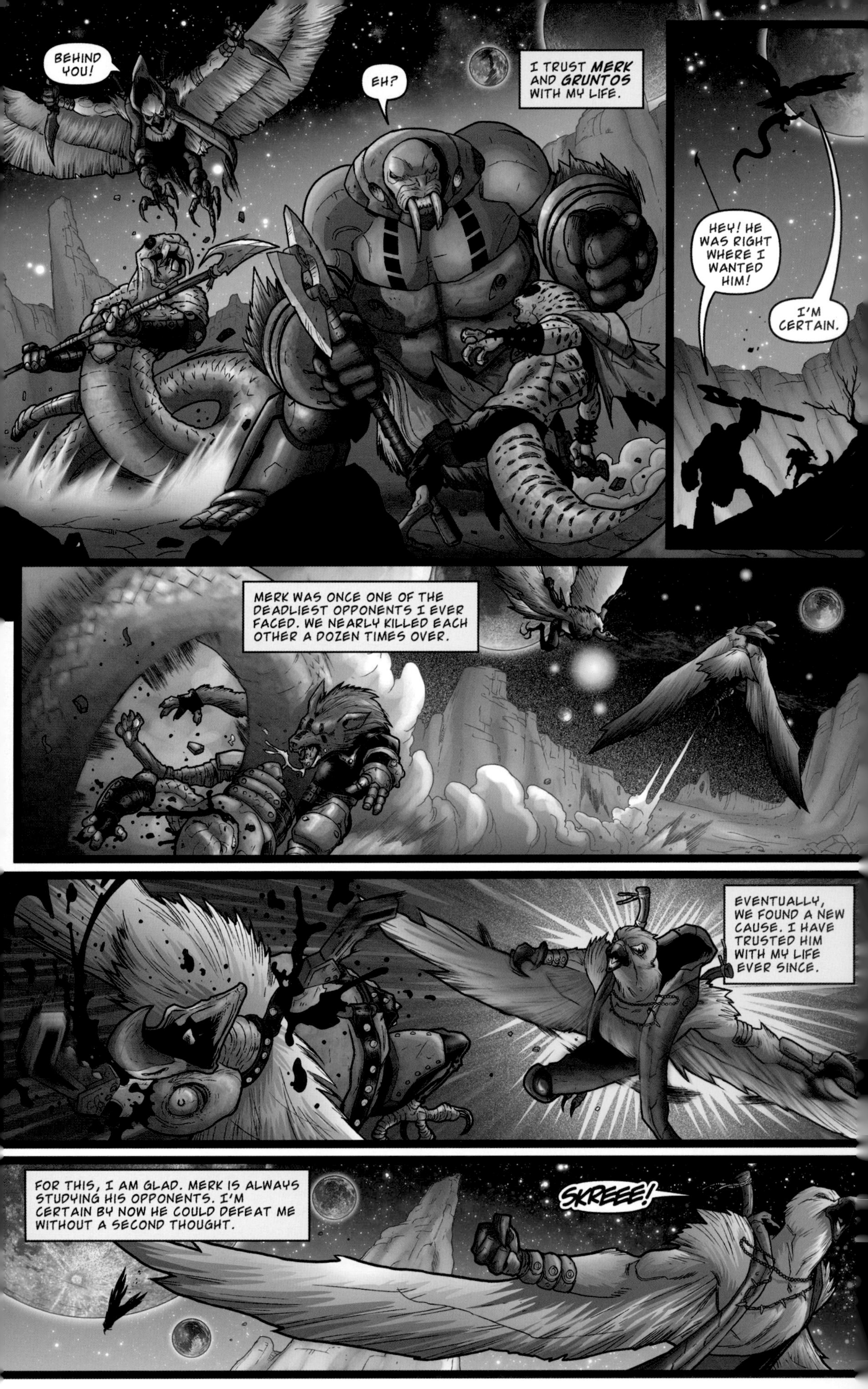
BEHIND YOU!
EH?
I TRUST MERK AND GRUNTOS WITH MY LIFE.
HEY! HE WAS RIGHT WHERE I WANTED HIM!
I'M CERTAIN.
MERK WAS ONCE ONE OF THE DEADLIEST OPPONENTS I EVER FACED. WE NEARLY KILLED EACH OTHER A DOZEN TIMES OVER.
EVENTUALLY, WE FOUND A NEW CAUSE. I HAVE TRUSTED HIM WITH MY LIFE EVER SINCE.
FOR THIS, I AM GLAD. MERK IS ALWAYS STUDYING HIS OPPONENTS. I'M CERTAIN BY NOW HE COULD DEFEAT ME WITHOUT A SECOND THOUGHT.
SKREEE!

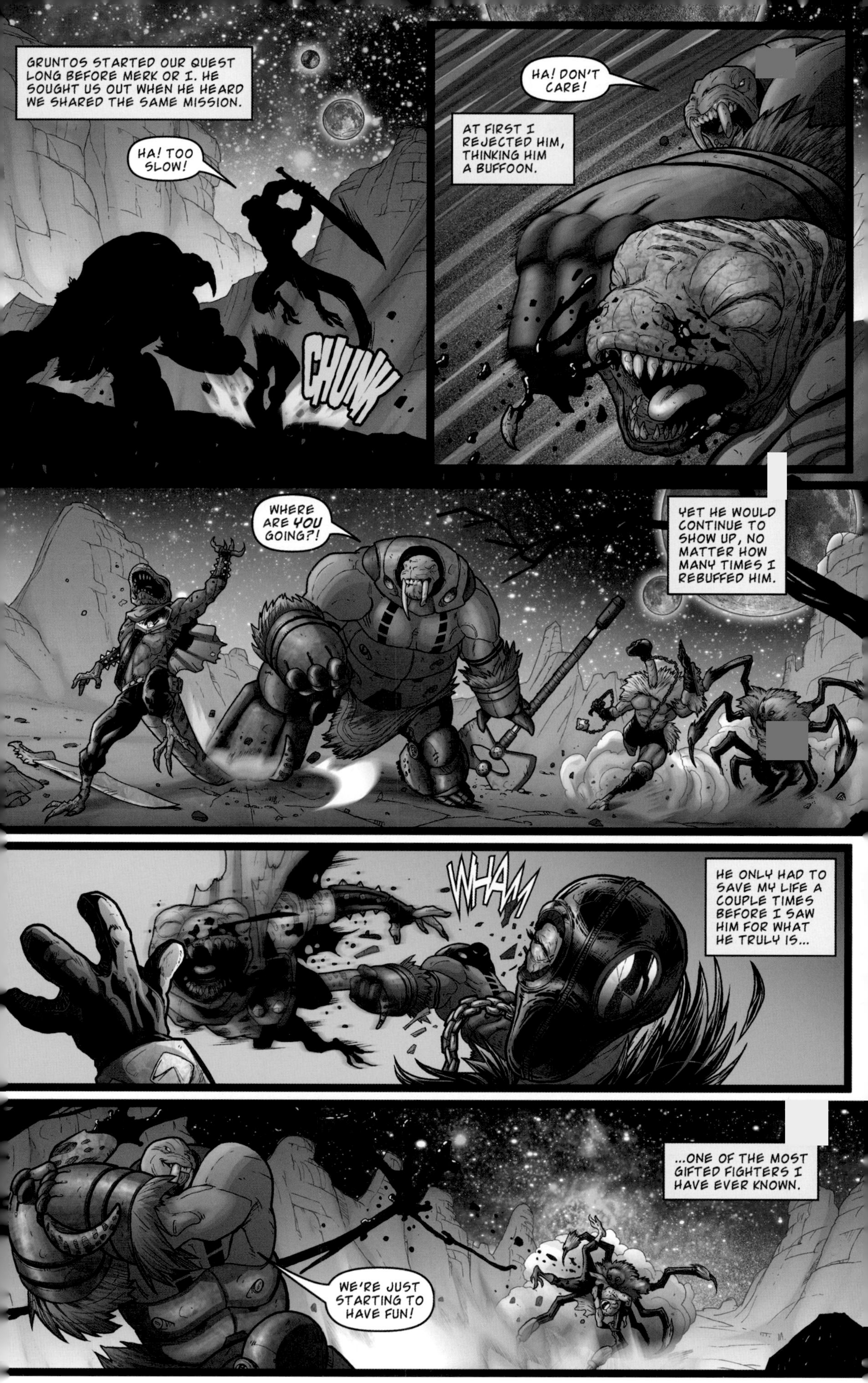
GRUNTOS STARTED OUR QUEST LONG BEFORE MERK OR I. HE SOUGHT US OUT WHEN HE HEARD WE SHARED THE SAME MISSION.
HA! TOO SLOW!
CHUNK
HA! DON'T CARE!
AT FIRST I REJECTED HIM, THINKING HIM A BUFFOON.
WHERE ARE *YOU* GOING?!
YET HE WOULD CONTINUE TO SHOW UP, NO MATTER HOW MANY TIMES I REBUFFED HIM.
WHAM
HE ONLY HAD TO SAVE MY LIFE A COUPLE TIMES BEFORE I SAW HIM FOR WHAT HE TRULY IS...
...ONE OF THE MOST GIFTED FIGHTERS I HAVE EVER KNOWN.
WE'RE JUST STARTING TO HAVE FUN!

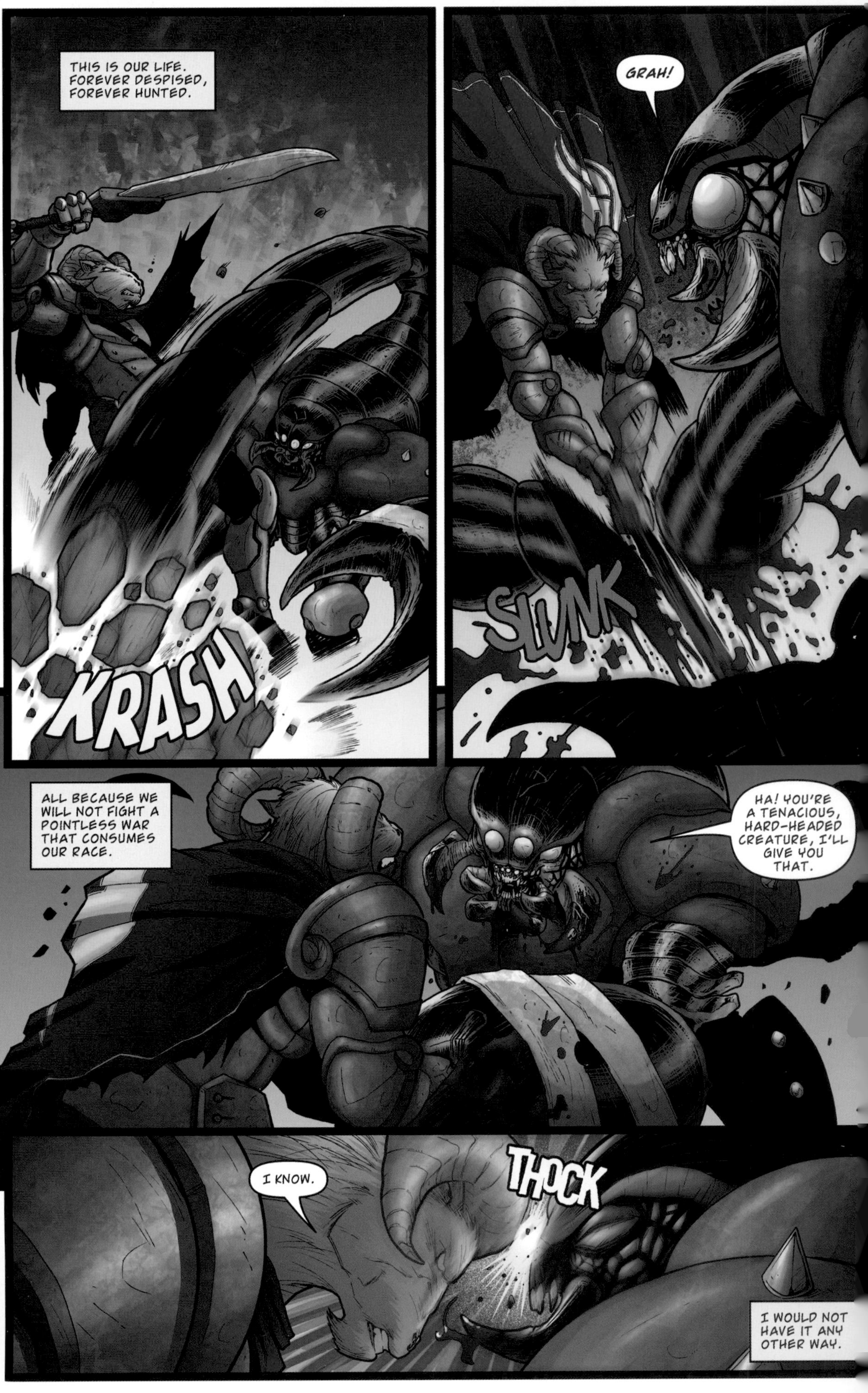
THIS IS OUR LIFE. FOREVER DESPISED, FOREVER HUNTED.
KRASH
GRAH!
SLUNK
ALL BECAUSE WE WILL NOT FIGHT A POINTLESS WAR THAT CONSUMES OUR RACE.
HA! YOU'RE A TENACIOUS, HARD-HEADED CREATURE, I'LL GIVE YOU THAT.
I KNOW.
THOCK
I WOULD NOT HAVE IT ANY OTHER WAY.

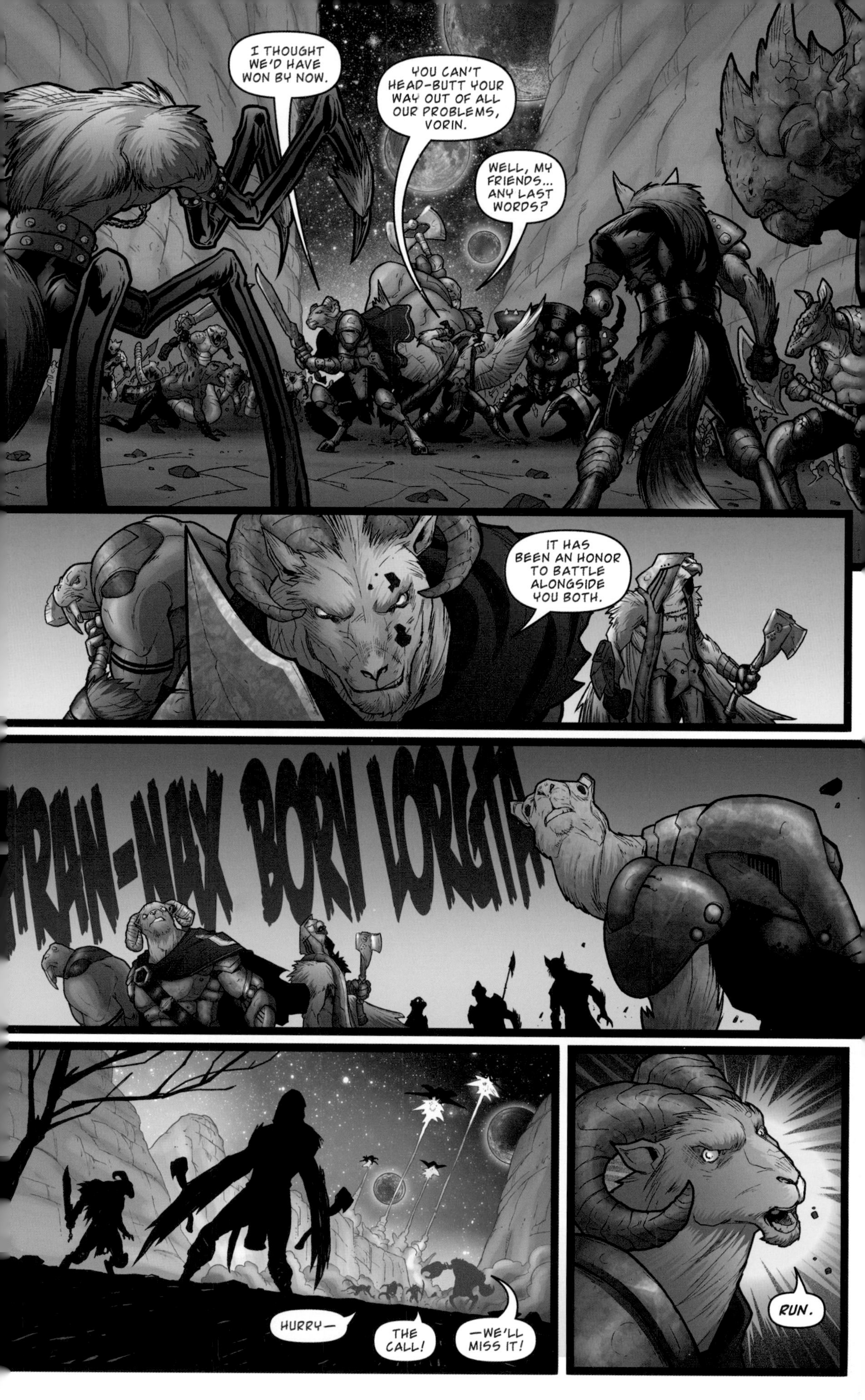
I THOUGHT WE'D HAVE WON BY NOW.
YOU CAN'T HEAD-BUTT YOUR WAY OUT OF ALL OUR PROBLEMS, VORIN.
WELL, MY FRIENDS... ANY LAST WORDS?
IT HAS BEEN AN HONOR TO BATTLE ALONGSIDE YOU BOTH.
HURRY—
THE CALL!
—WE'LL MISS IT!
RUN.

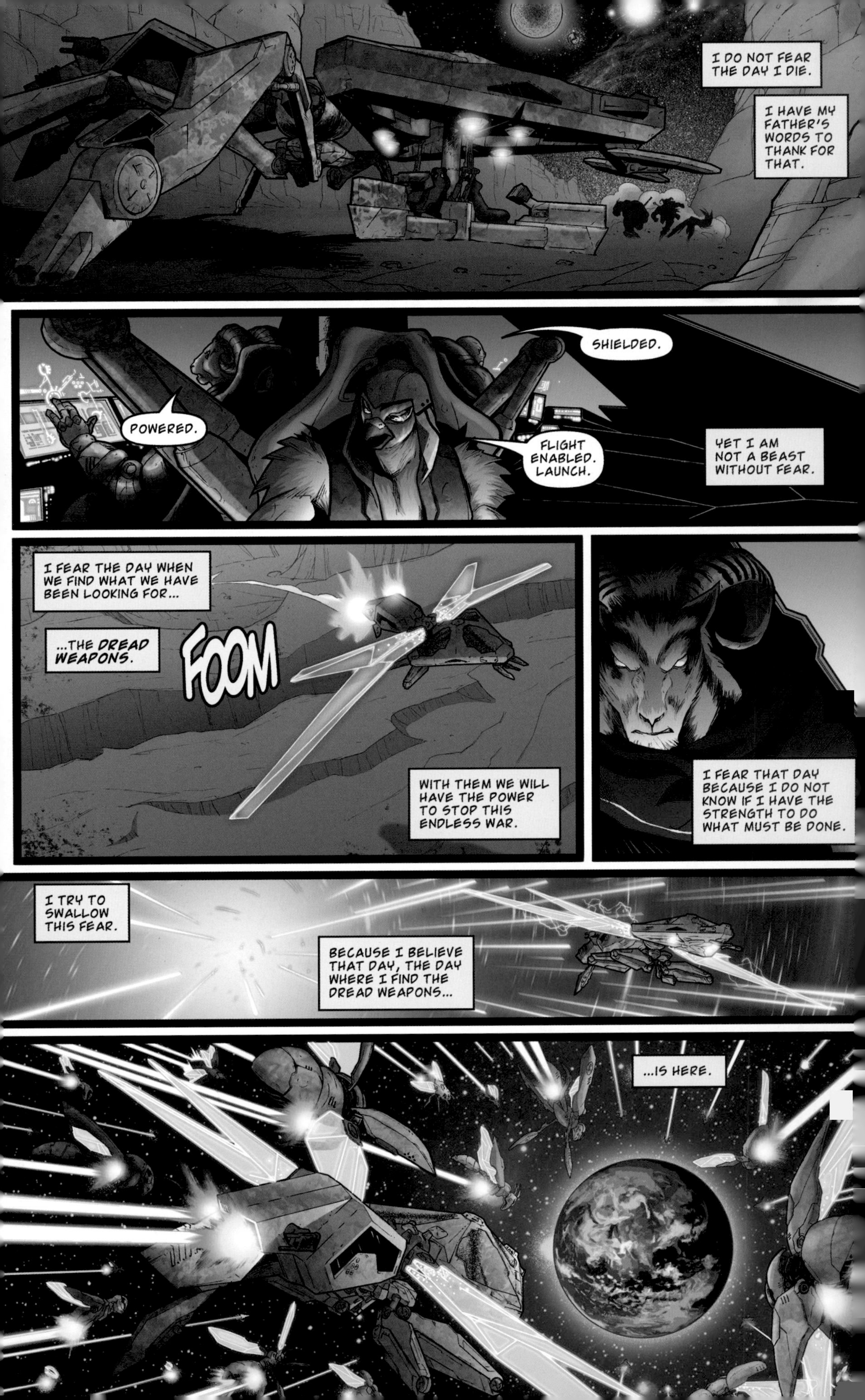
I DO NOT FEAR THE DAY I DIE.
I HAVE MY FATHER'S WORDS TO THANK FOR THAT.
SHIELDED.
POWERED.
FLIGHT ENABLED. LAUNCH.
YET I AM NOT A BEAST WITHOUT FEAR.
I FEAR THE DAY WHEN WE FIND WHAT WE HAVE BEEN LOOKING FOR...
...THE *DREAD WEAPONS*.
FOOM
WITH THEM WE WILL HAVE THE POWER TO STOP THIS ENDLESS WAR.
I FEAR THAT DAY BECAUSE I DO NOT KNOW IF I HAVE THE STRENGTH TO DO WHAT MUST BE DONE.
I TRY TO SWALLOW THIS FEAR.
BECAUSE I BELIEVE THAT DAY, THE DAY WHERE I FIND THE DREAD WEAPONS...
...IS HERE.

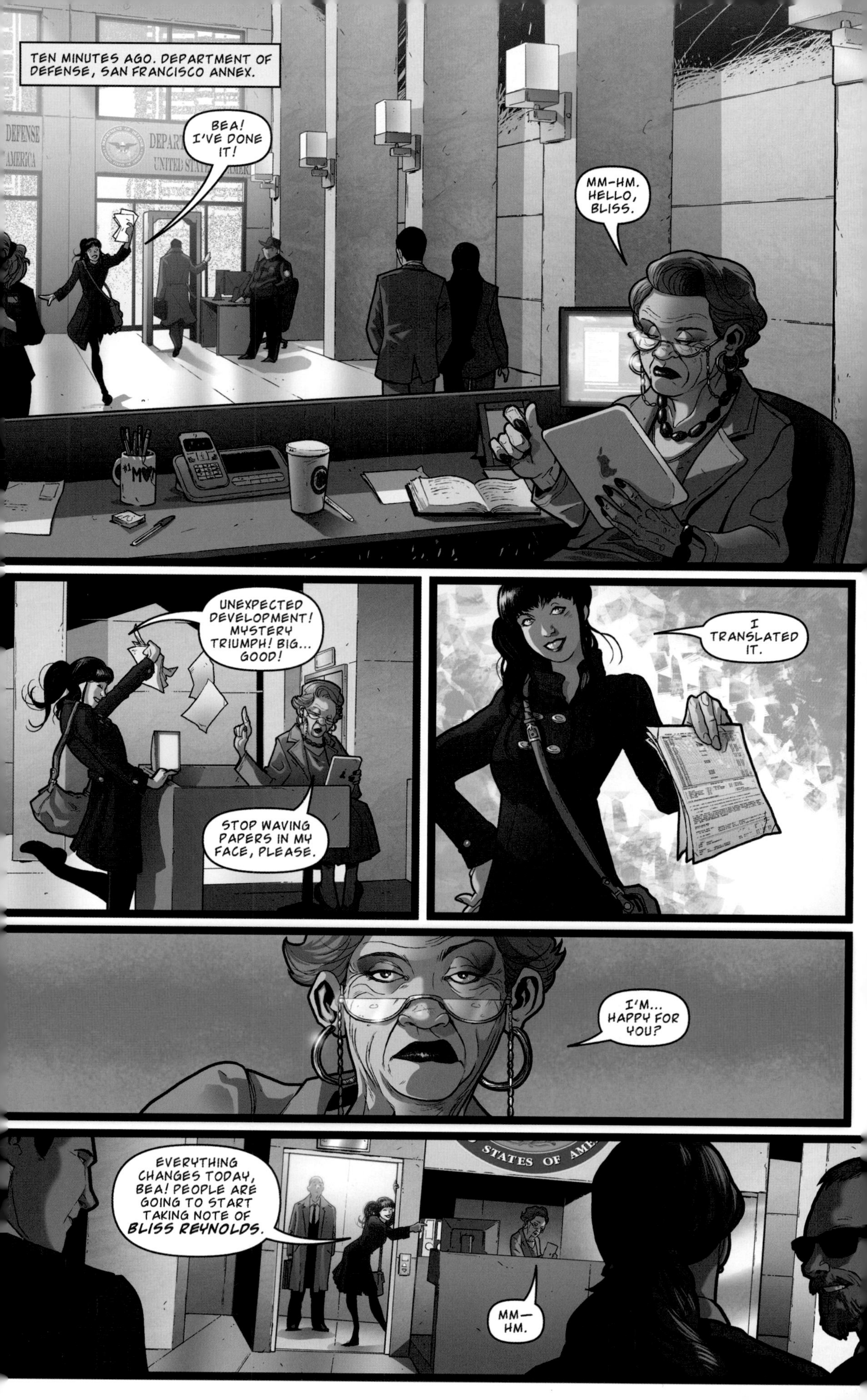
TEN MINUTES AGO. DEPARTMENT OF DEFENSE, SAN FRANCISCO ANNEX.
BEA! I'VE DONE IT!
MM-HM. HELLO, BLISS.
UNEXPECTED DEVELOPMENT! MYSTERY TRIUMPH! BIG... GOOD!
STOP WAVING PAPERS IN MY FACE, PLEASE.
I TRANSLATED IT.
I'M... HAPPY FOR YOU?
EVERYTHING CHANGES TODAY, BEA! PEOPLE ARE GOING TO START TAKING NOTE OF ***BLISS REYNOLDS***.
MM— HM.

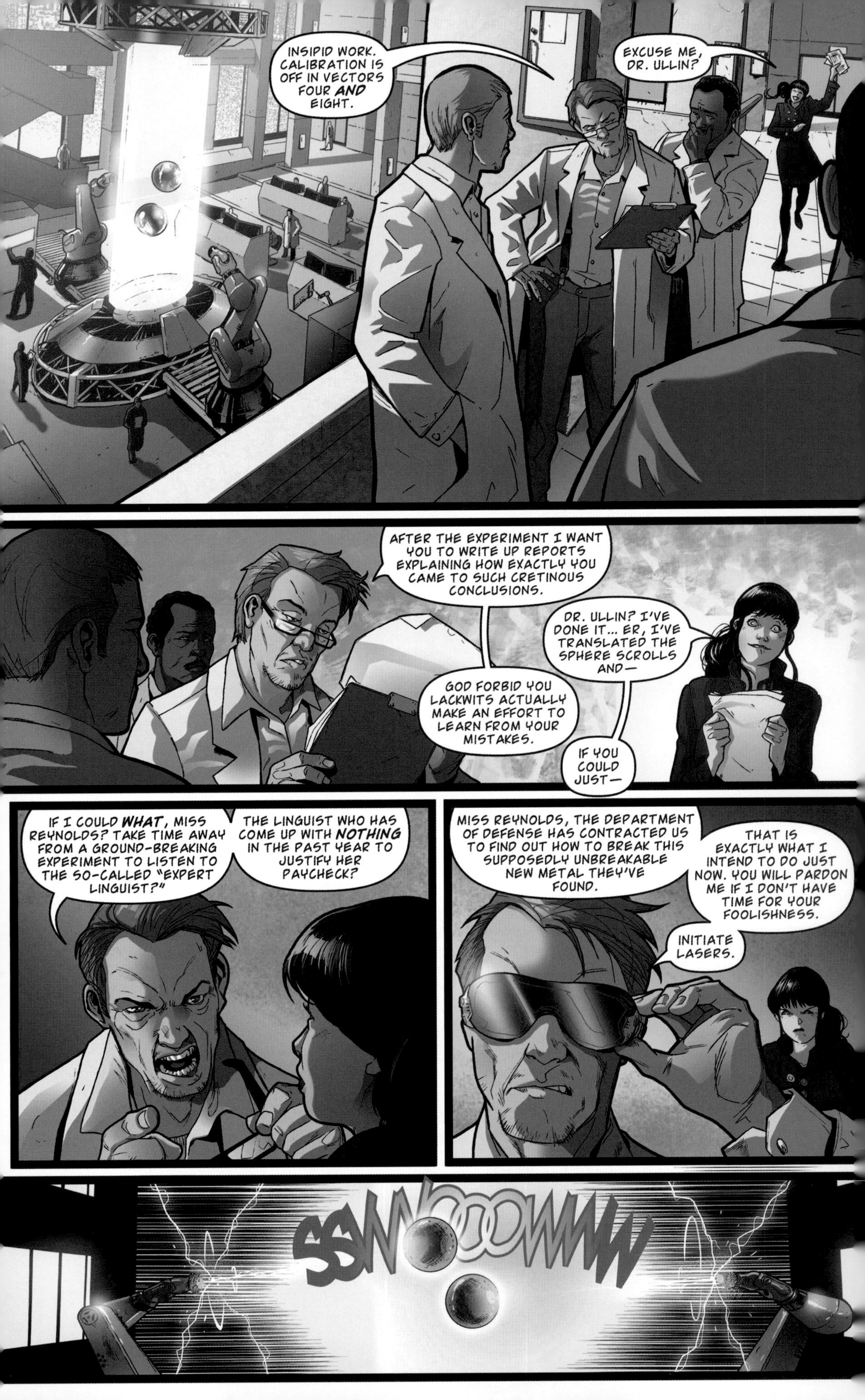
INSIPID WORK. CALIBRATION IS OFF IN VECTORS FOUR AND EIGHT.
EXCUSE ME, DR. ULLIN?
AFTER THE EXPERIMENT I WANT YOU TO WRITE UP REPORTS EXPLAINING HOW EXACTLY YOU CAME TO SUCH CRETINOUS CONCLUSIONS.
DR. ULLIN? I'VE DONE IT... ER, I'VE TRANSLATED THE SPHERE SCROLLS AND—
GOD FORBID YOU LACKWITS ACTUALLY MAKE AN EFFORT TO LEARN FROM YOUR MISTAKES.
IF YOU COULD JUST—
IF I COULD WHAT, MISS REYNOLDS? TAKE TIME AWAY FROM A GROUND-BREAKING EXPERIMENT TO LISTEN TO THE SO-CALLED "EXPERT LINGUIST?"
THE LINGUIST WHO HAS COME UP WITH NOTHING IN THE PAST YEAR TO JUSTIFY HER PAYCHECK?
MISS REYNOLDS, THE DEPARTMENT OF DEFENSE HAS CONTRACTED US TO FIND OUT HOW TO BREAK THIS SUPPOSEDLY UNBREAKABLE NEW METAL THEY'VE FOUND.
THAT IS EXACTLY WHAT I INTEND TO DO JUST NOW. YOU WILL PARDON ME IF I DON'T HAVE TIME FOR YOUR FOOLISHNESS.
INITIATE LASERS.
SSWOOOWWW

THEY'RE UNBREAKABLE. THEY'RE @#$% UNBREAKABLE.

THEY'RE NOT MEANT TO BE BROKEN. THEY'RE MEANT TO BE OPENED.

WHAT ON EARTH ARE YOU YAMMERING ABOUT, YOU STUPID GIRL?

I'VE BEEN TRYING TO TELL YOU. I'VE TRANSLATED THE UNKNOWN LANGUAGE IN THE SCROLLS THAT WERE FOUND WITH THE SPHERES.

IT ALL CENTERS ON ONE PHRASE, REPEATED SEVERAL TIMES. ONCE I CRACKED THAT, EVERYTHING FELL INTO PLACE. FROM WHAT I CAN TELL, THIS PHRASE IS MEANT TO OPEN THE SPHERES AND INITIATE SOME SORT OF RITUAL... CEREMONIAL, I CAN ONLY IMAGINE—

BLISS. THE POINT. WHAT IS THE PHRASE?

WELL, IN ENGLISH, IT MEANS "TO BATTLE, WE BEASTS." IN THE ORIGINAL LANGUAGE I THINK IT WAS PRONOUNCED...

..."THRAN-NAX BORV LORGTA."

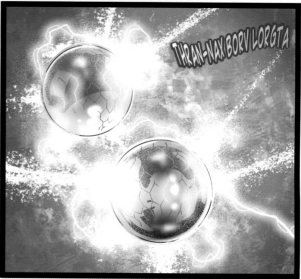

THRAN-NAX BORV LORGTA

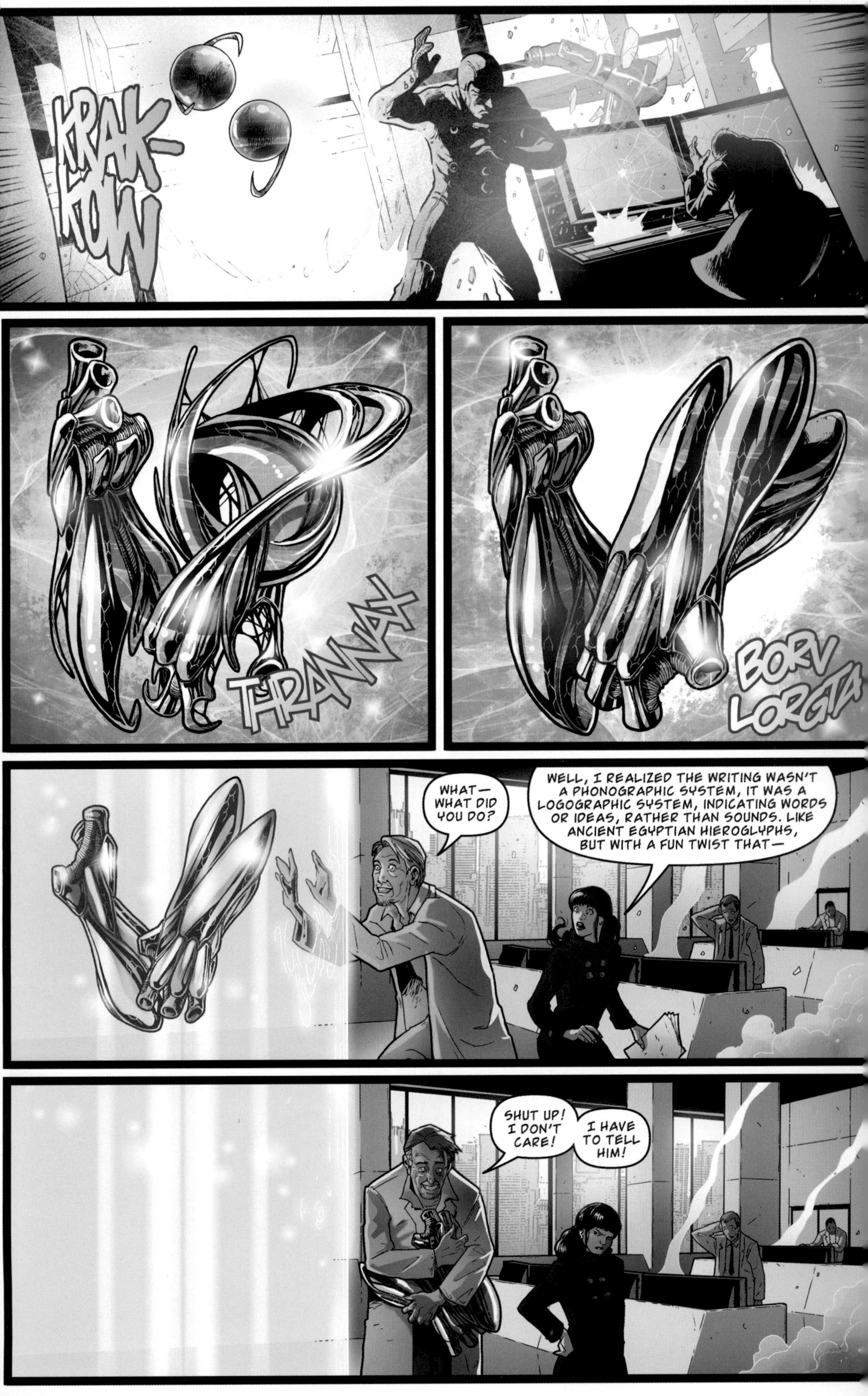
KRAK-KOW
THRANNAX
BORV LORGTA
WHAT— WHAT DID YOU DO?
WELL, I REALIZED THE WRITING WASN'T A PHONOGRAPHIC SYSTEM, IT WAS A LOGOGRAPHIC SYSTEM, INDICATING WORDS OR IDEAS, RATHER THAN SOUNDS. LIKE ANCIENT EGYPTIAN HIEROGLYPHS, BUT WITH A FUN TWIST THAT—
SHUT UP! I DON'T CARE!
I HAVE TO TELL HIM!

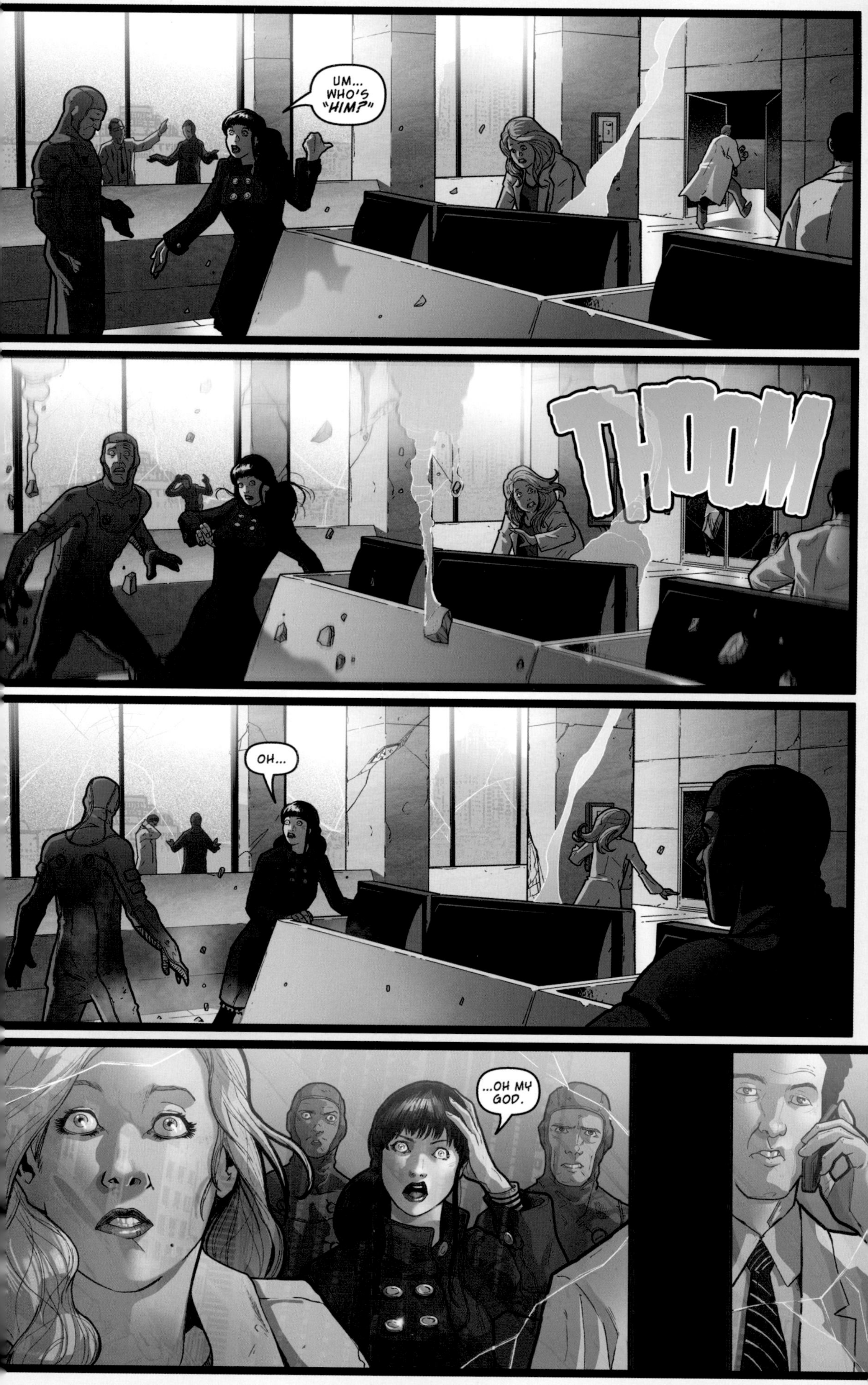
UM... WHO'S "HIM?"
THOOM
OH...
...OH MY GOD.

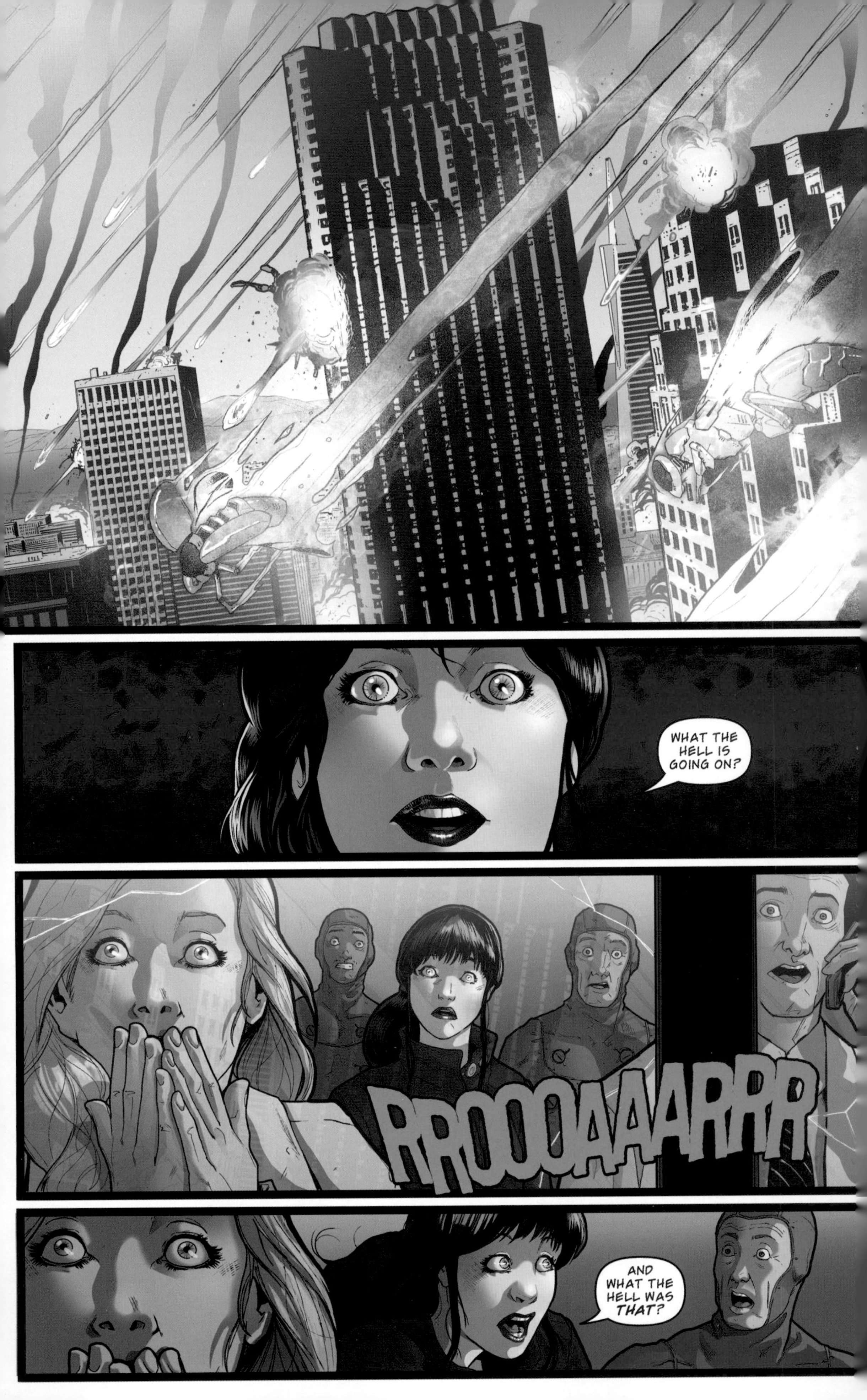
WHAT THE HELL IS GOING ON?
RROOOAAARRR
AND WHAT THE HELL WAS THAT?

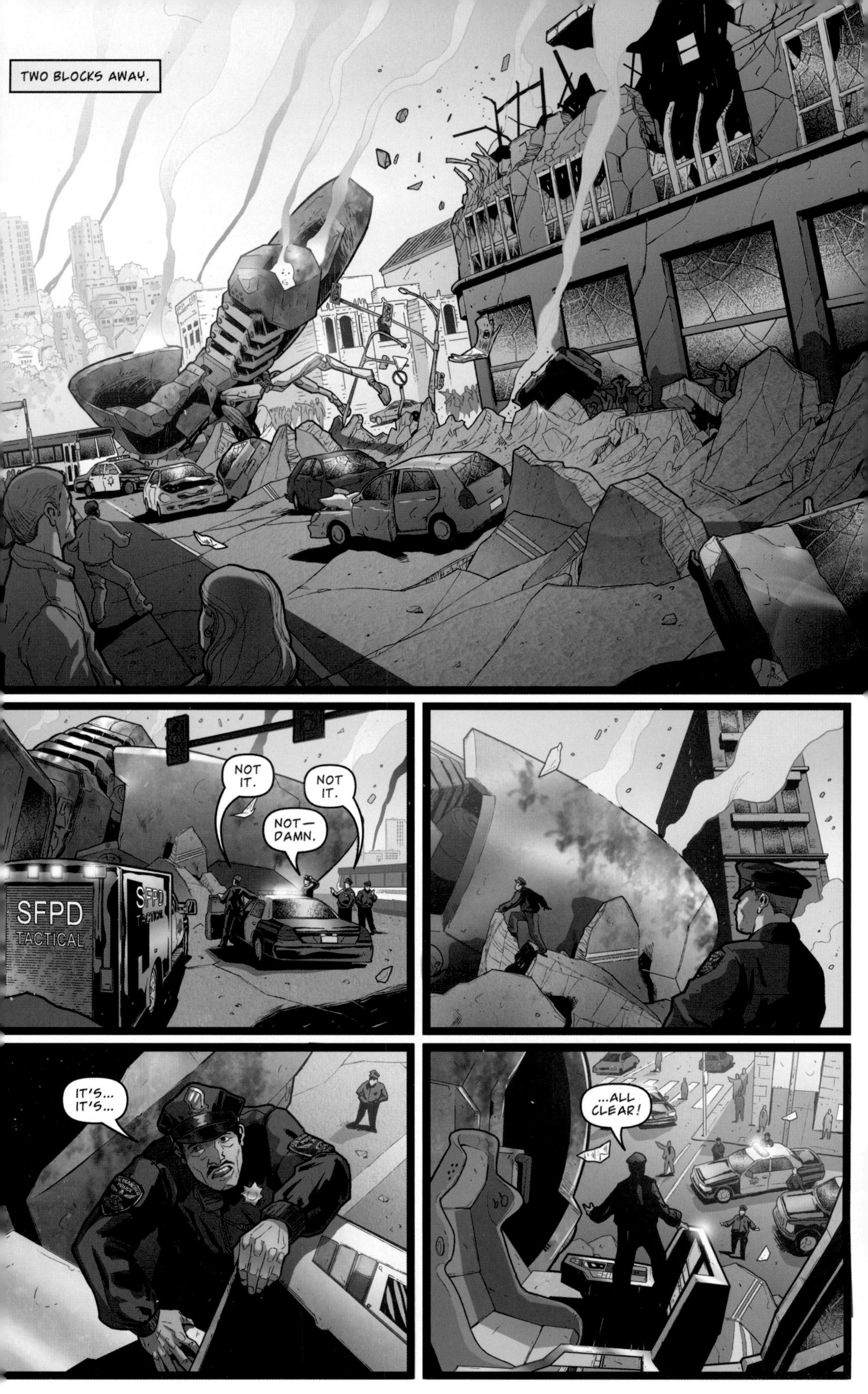
TWO BLOCKS AWAY.
NOT IT.
NOT IT.
NOT— DAMN.
SFPD TACTICAL
SFPD TACTICAL
IT'S... IT'S...
...ALL CLEAR!

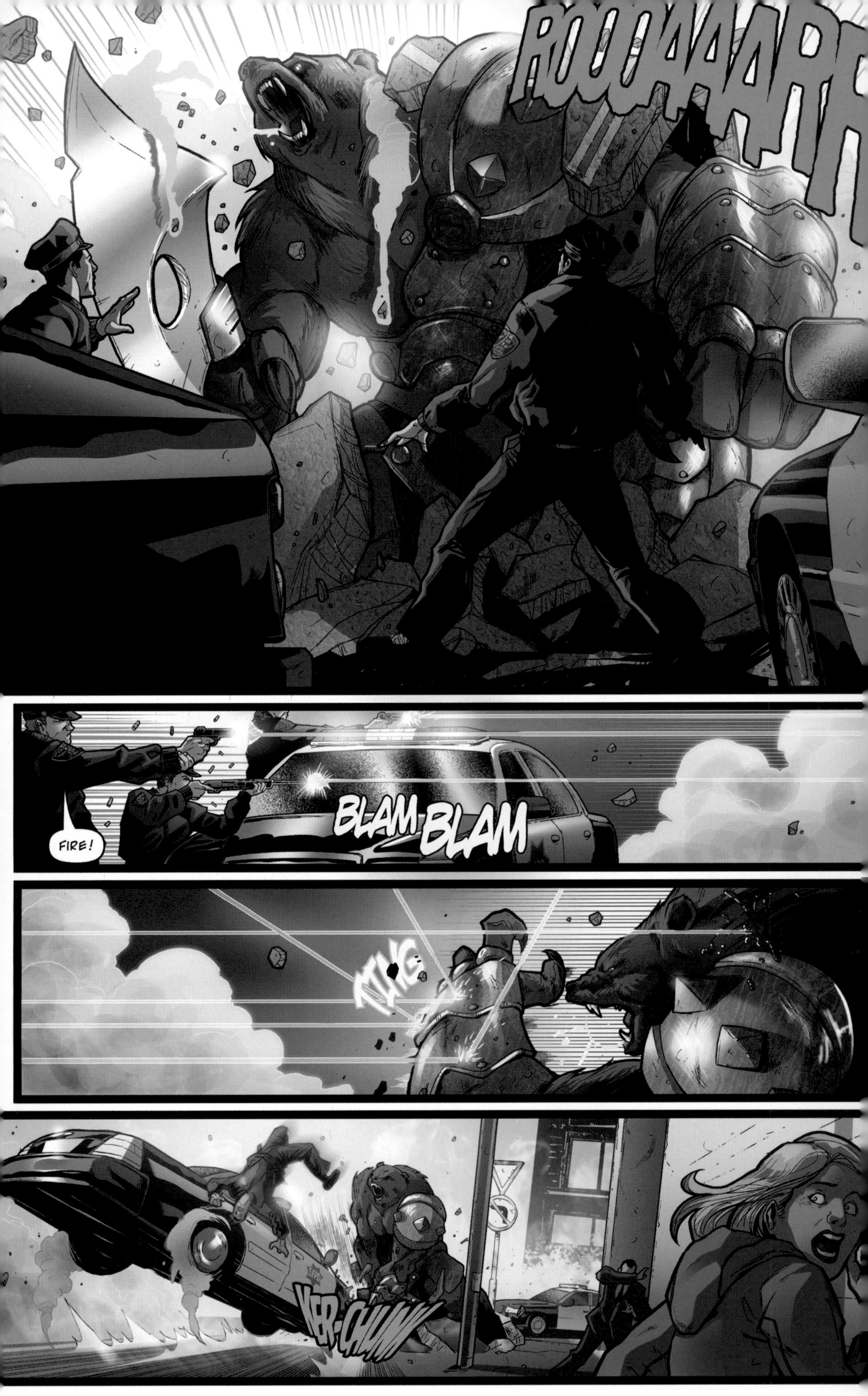

ROOOAAARR
FIRE!
BLAM BLAM
TING
SFPD
KER-CHUNK

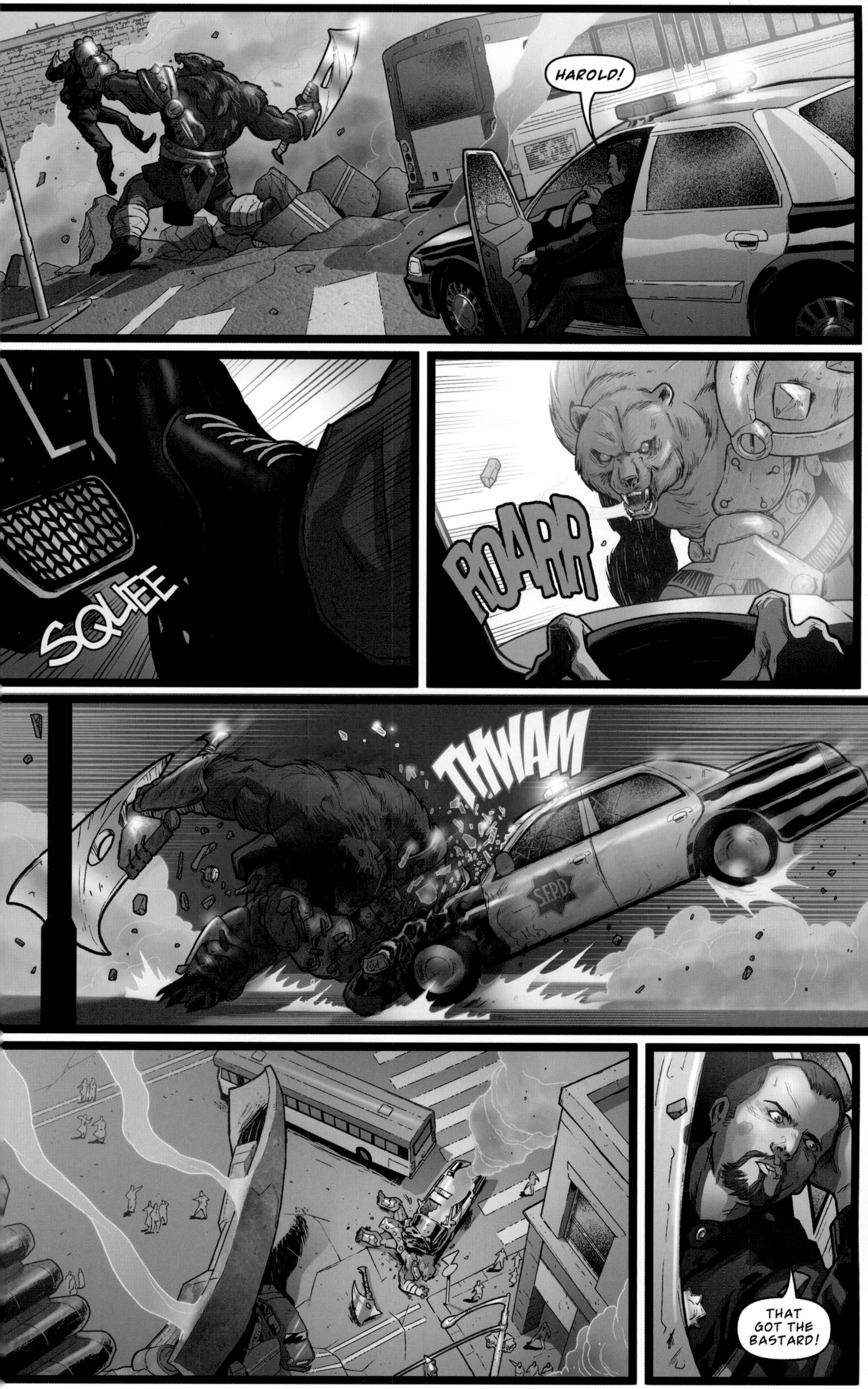
HAROLD!
SQUEE
ROARR
THWAM
S.F.P.D.
THAT GOT THE BASTARD!

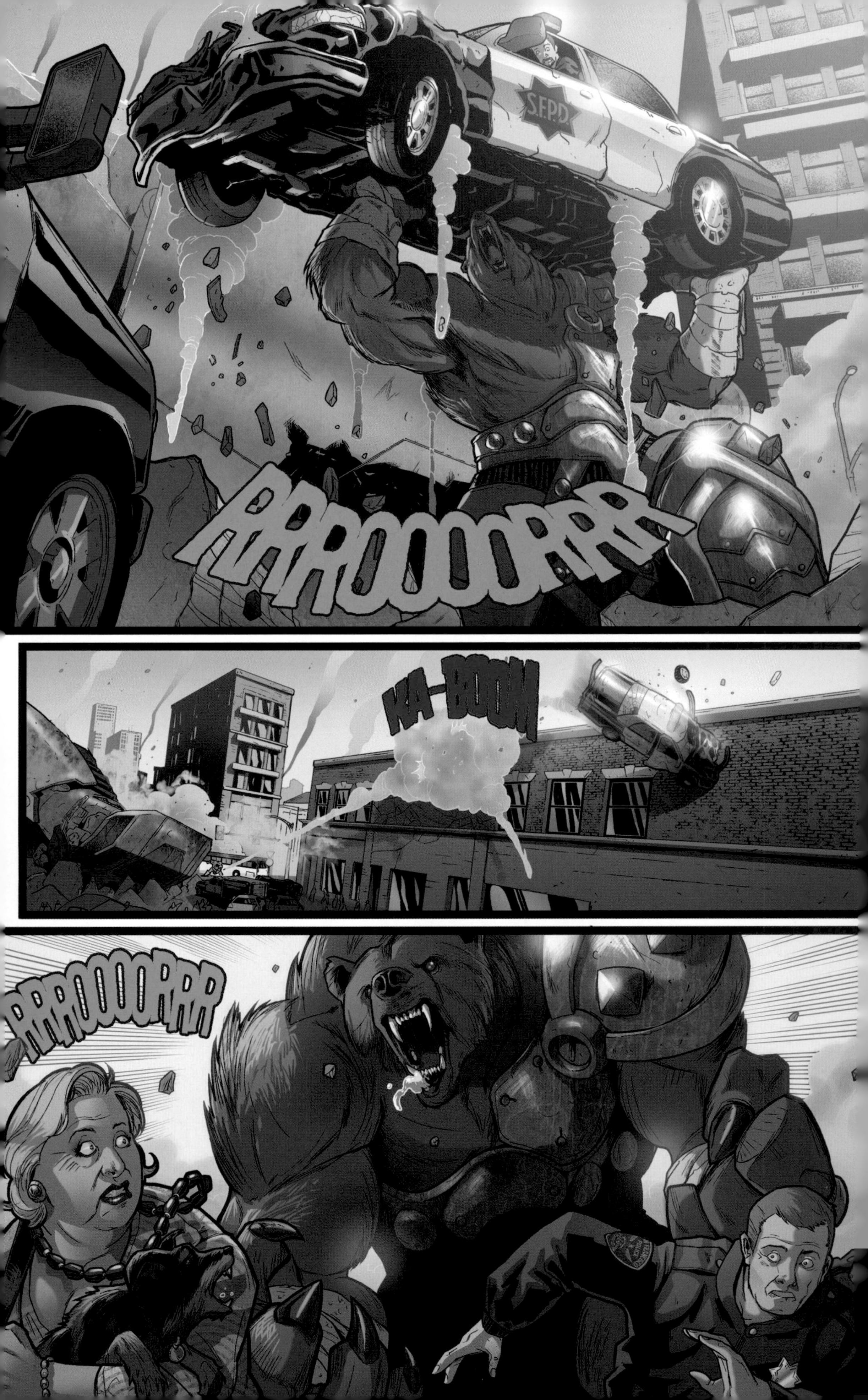
RRRROOOOORRR
S.F.P.D.
KA-BOOM
RRRROOOORRR

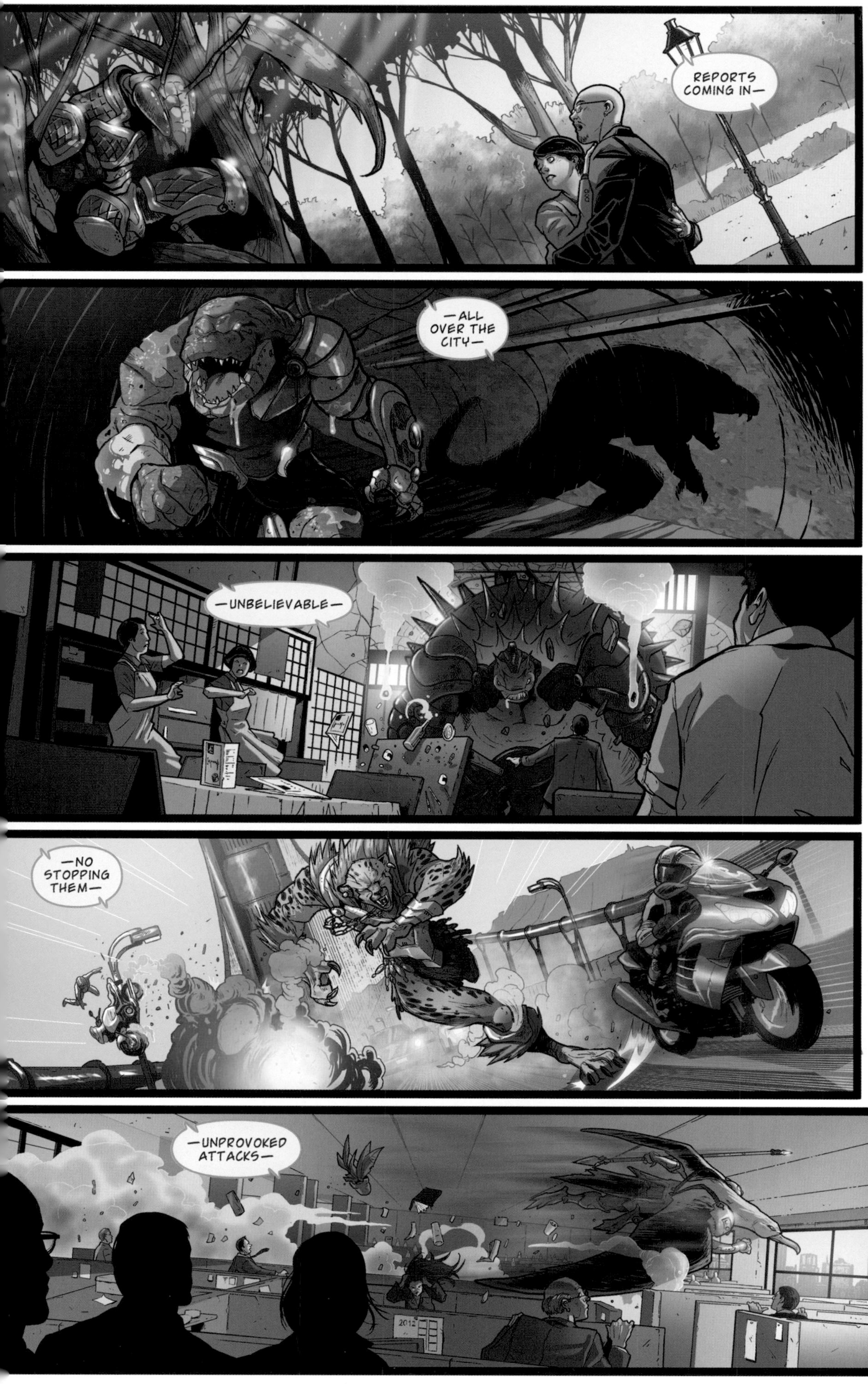
REPORTS COMING IN—
—ALL OVER THE CITY—
—UNBELIEVABLE—
—NO STOPPING THEM—
—UNPROVOKED ATTACKS—

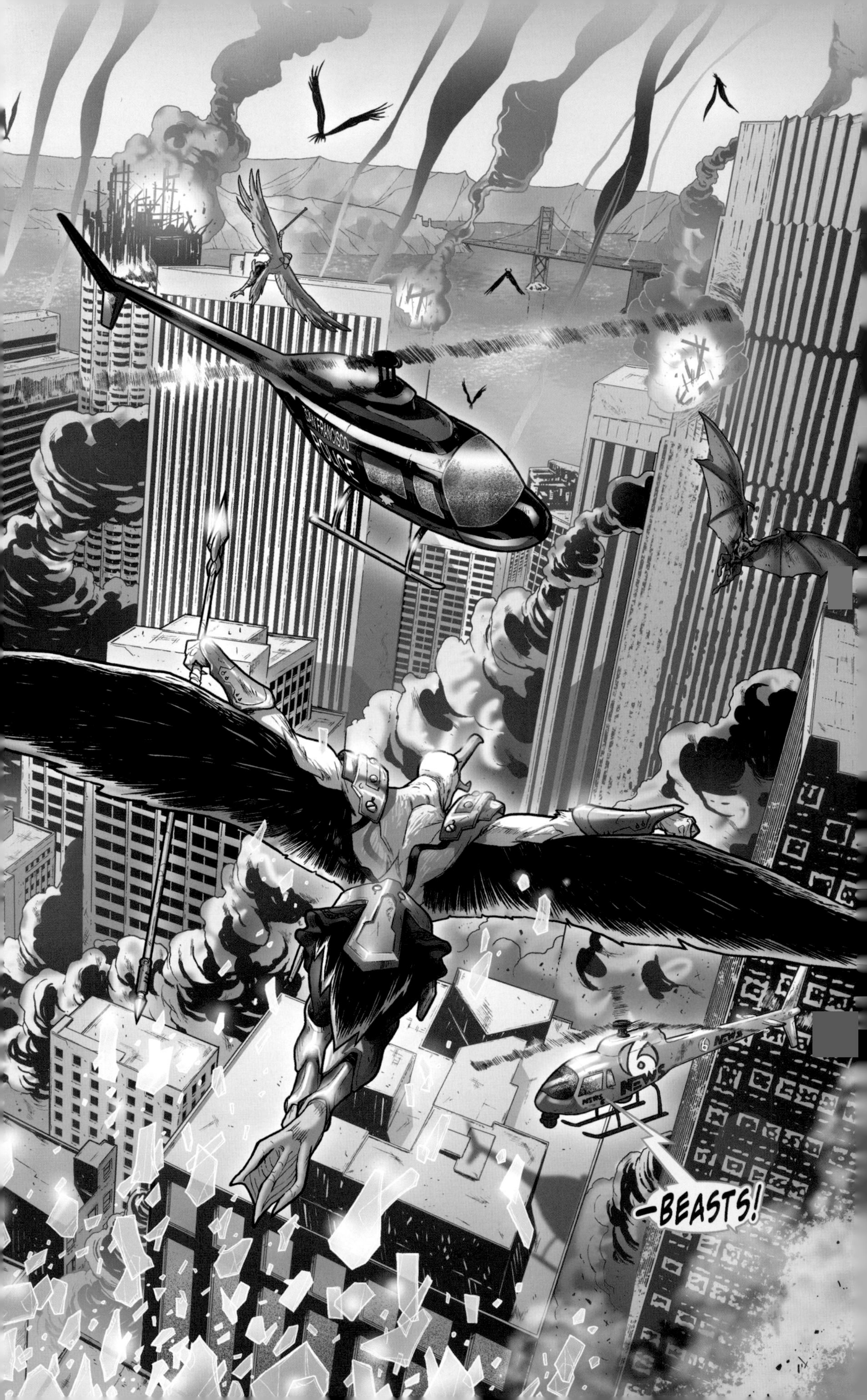
SAN FRANCISCO
POLICE
NEWS
—BEASTS!

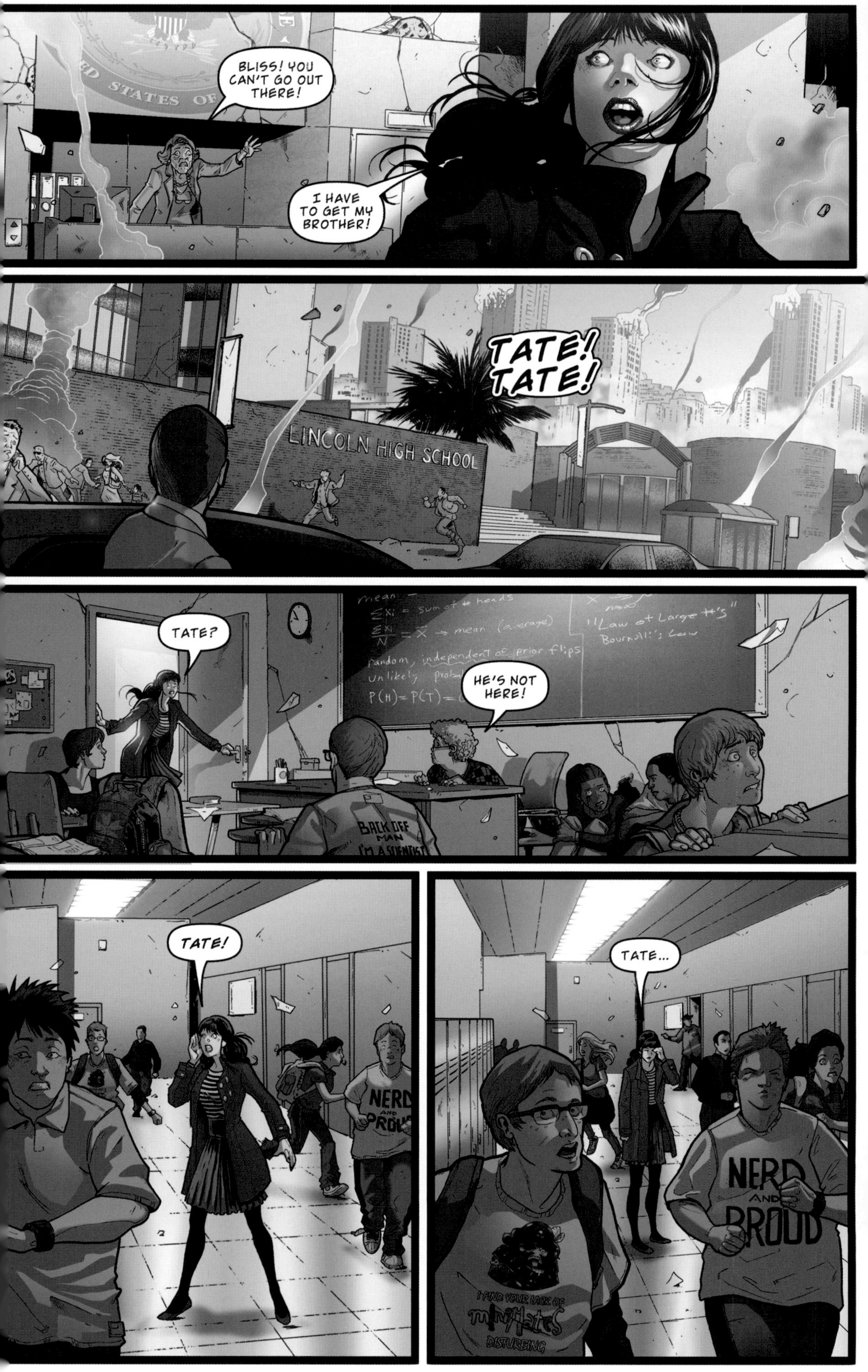
BLISS! YOU CAN'T GO OUT THERE!
I HAVE TO GET MY BROTHER!
TATE! TATE!
LINCOLN HIGH SCHOOL
TATE?
random, independent of prior flips
"Law of Large #'s"
HE'S NOT HERE!
BACK OFF MAN
TATE!
NERD AND PROUD
TATE...
NERD AND PROUD
DISTURBING

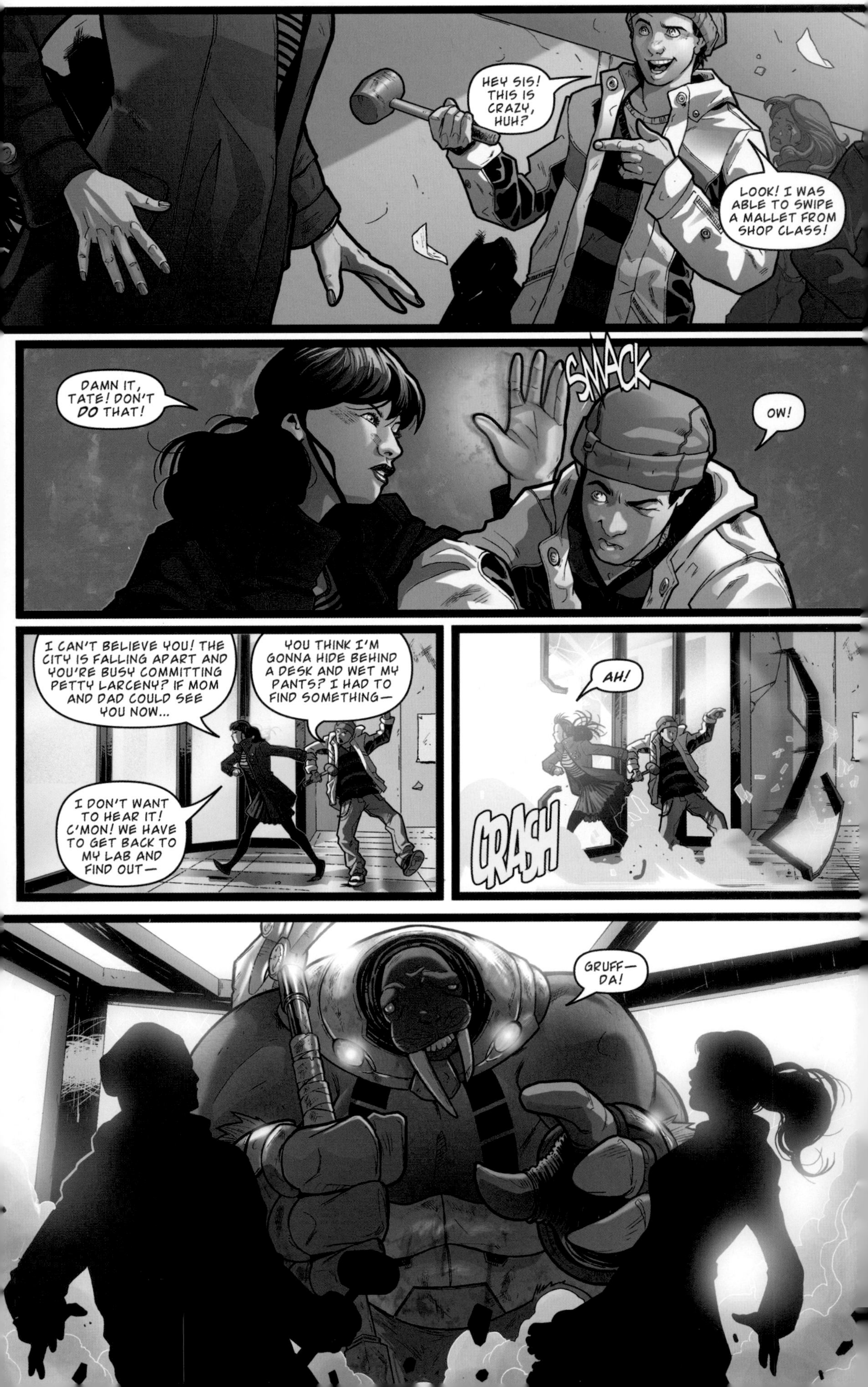
HEY SIS! THIS IS CRAZY, HUH?
LOOK! I WAS ABLE TO SWIPE A MALLET FROM SHOP CLASS!
SMACK
DAMN IT, TATE! DON'T DO THAT!
OW!
I CAN'T BELIEVE YOU! THE CITY IS FALLING APART AND YOU'RE BUSY COMMITTING PETTY LARCENY? IF MOM AND DAD COULD SEE YOU NOW...
YOU THINK I'M GONNA HIDE BEHIND A DESK AND WET MY PANTS? I HAD TO FIND SOMETHING—
I DON'T WANT TO HEAR IT! C'MON! WE HAVE TO GET BACK TO MY LAB AND FIND OUT—
AH!
CRASH
GRUFF—DA!

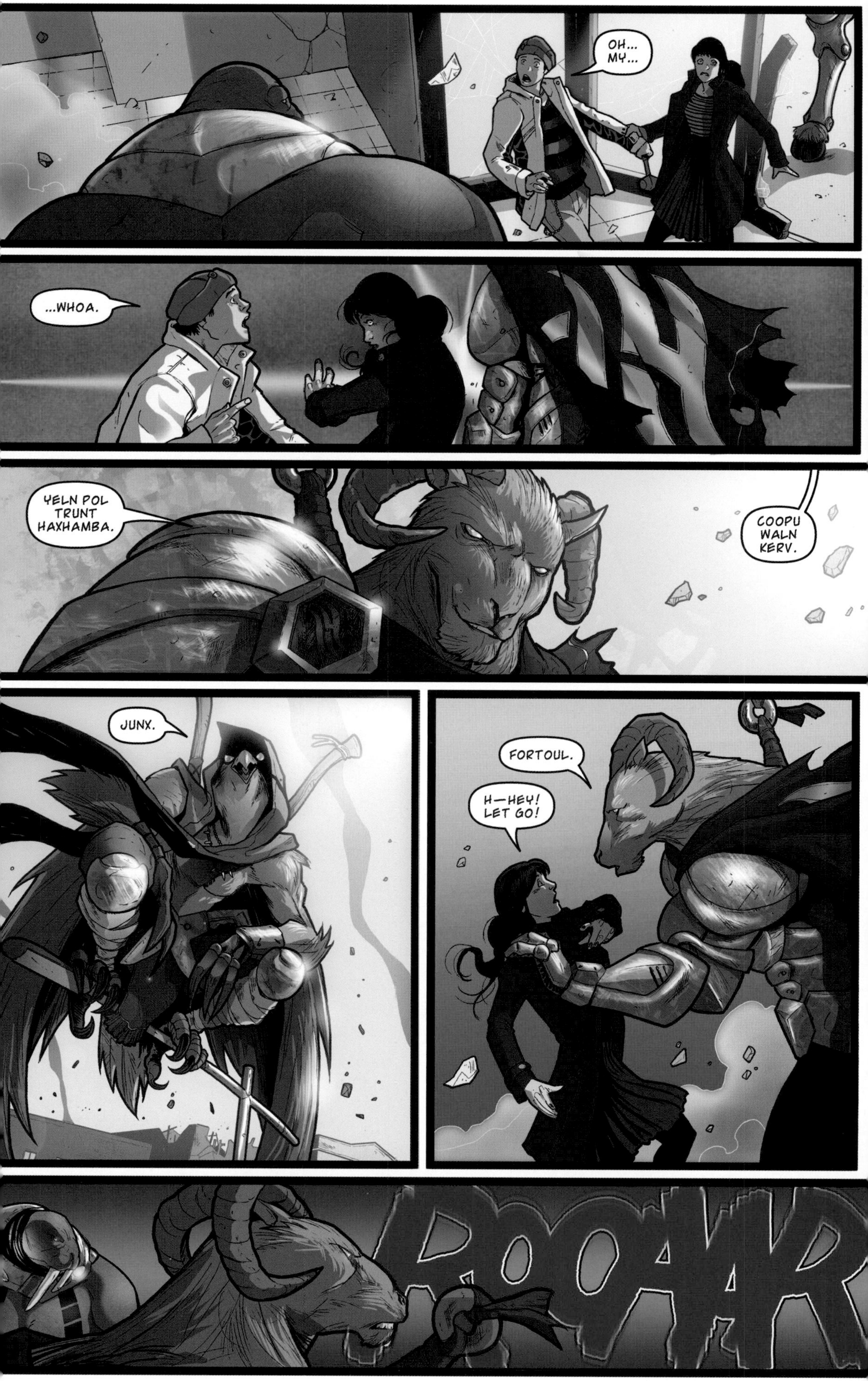
OH... MY...
...WHOA.
YELN POL TRUNT HAXHAMBA.
COOPU WALN KERV.
JUNX.
FORTOUL.
H—HEY! LET GO!
ROOAAR

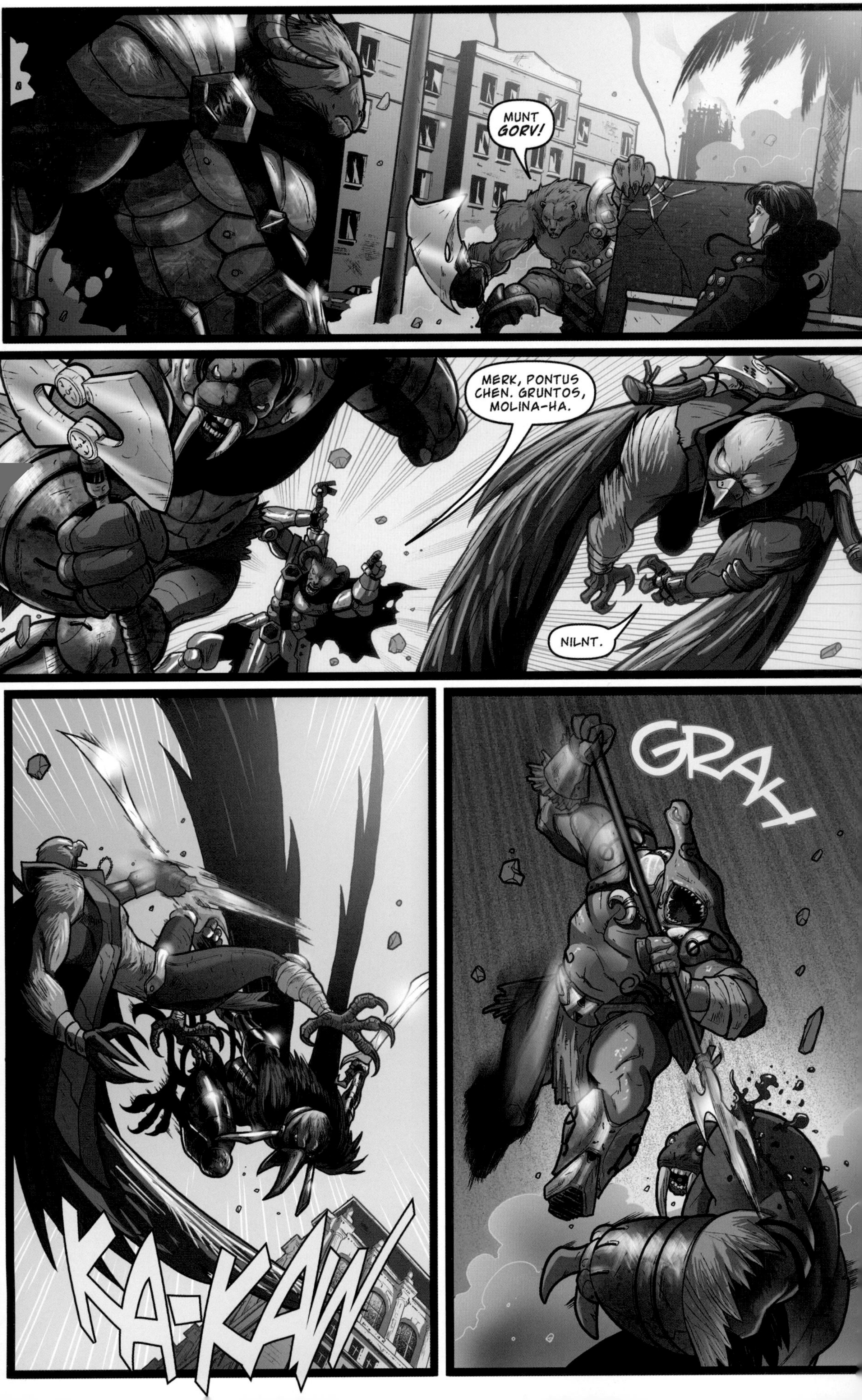
MUNT GORV!
MERK, PONTUS CHEN. GRUNTOS, MOLINA-HA.
NILNT.
KA-KAW
GRAH

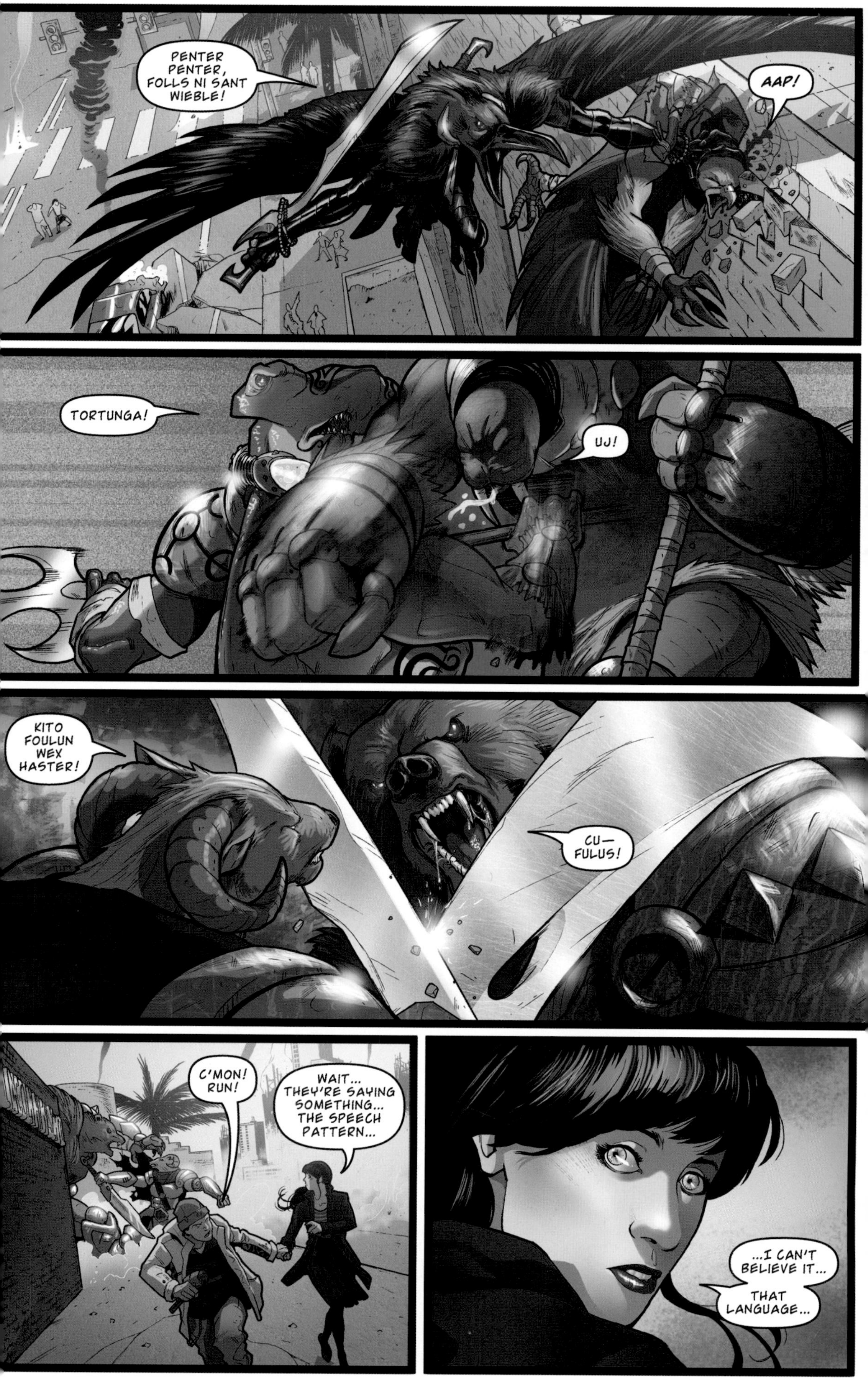
PENTER PENTER, FOLLS NI SANT WIEBLE!
AAP!
TORTUNGA!
UJ!
KITO FOULUN WEX HASTER!
CU-FULUS!
C'MON! RUN!
WAIT... THEY'RE SAYING SOMETHING... THE SPEECH PATTERN...
...I CAN'T BELIEVE IT...
THAT LANGUAGE...

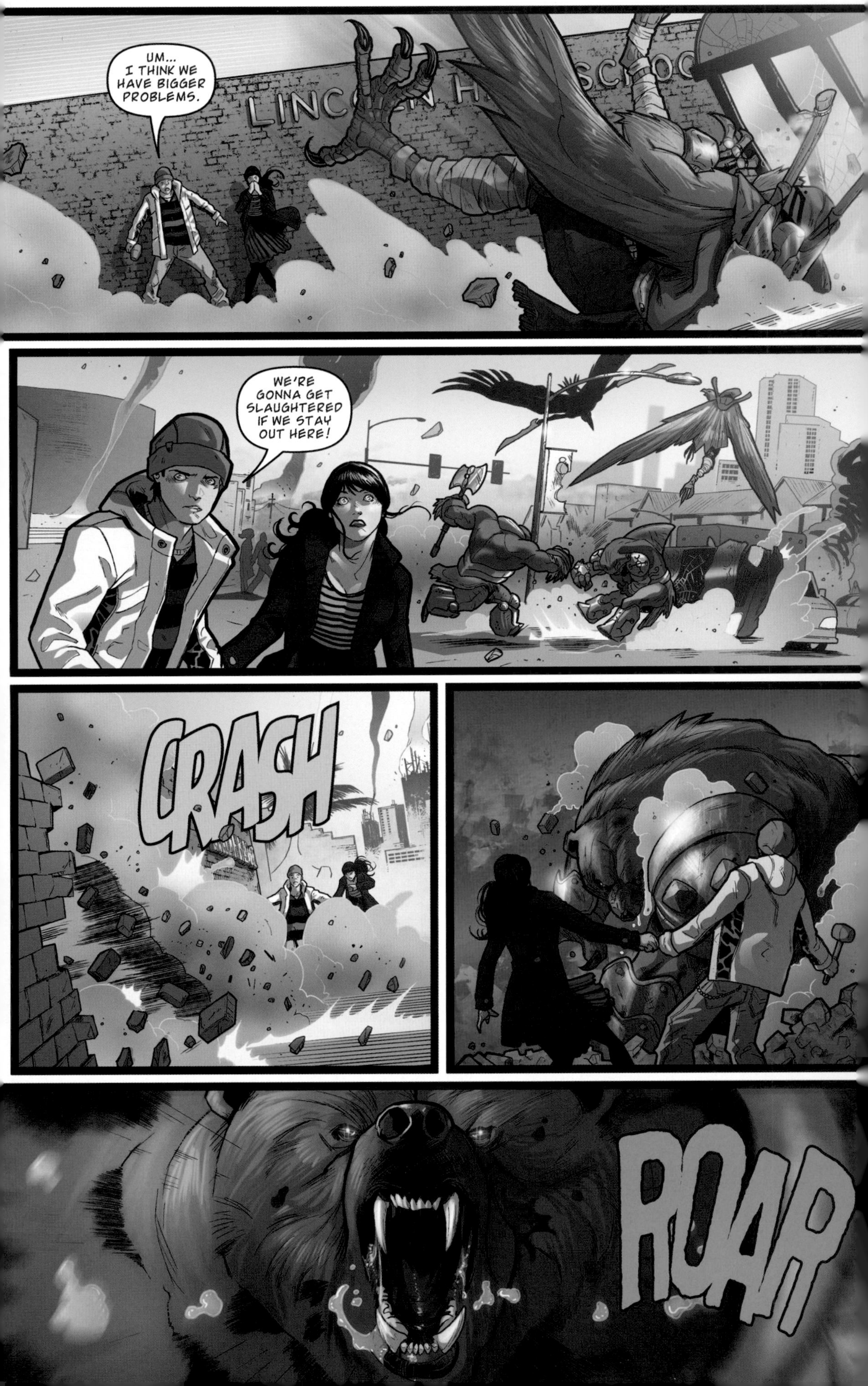
UM... I THINK WE HAVE BIGGER PROBLEMS.
LINCOLN H SCHOO
WE'RE GONNA GET SLAUGHTERED IF WE STAY OUT HERE!
CRASH
ROAR

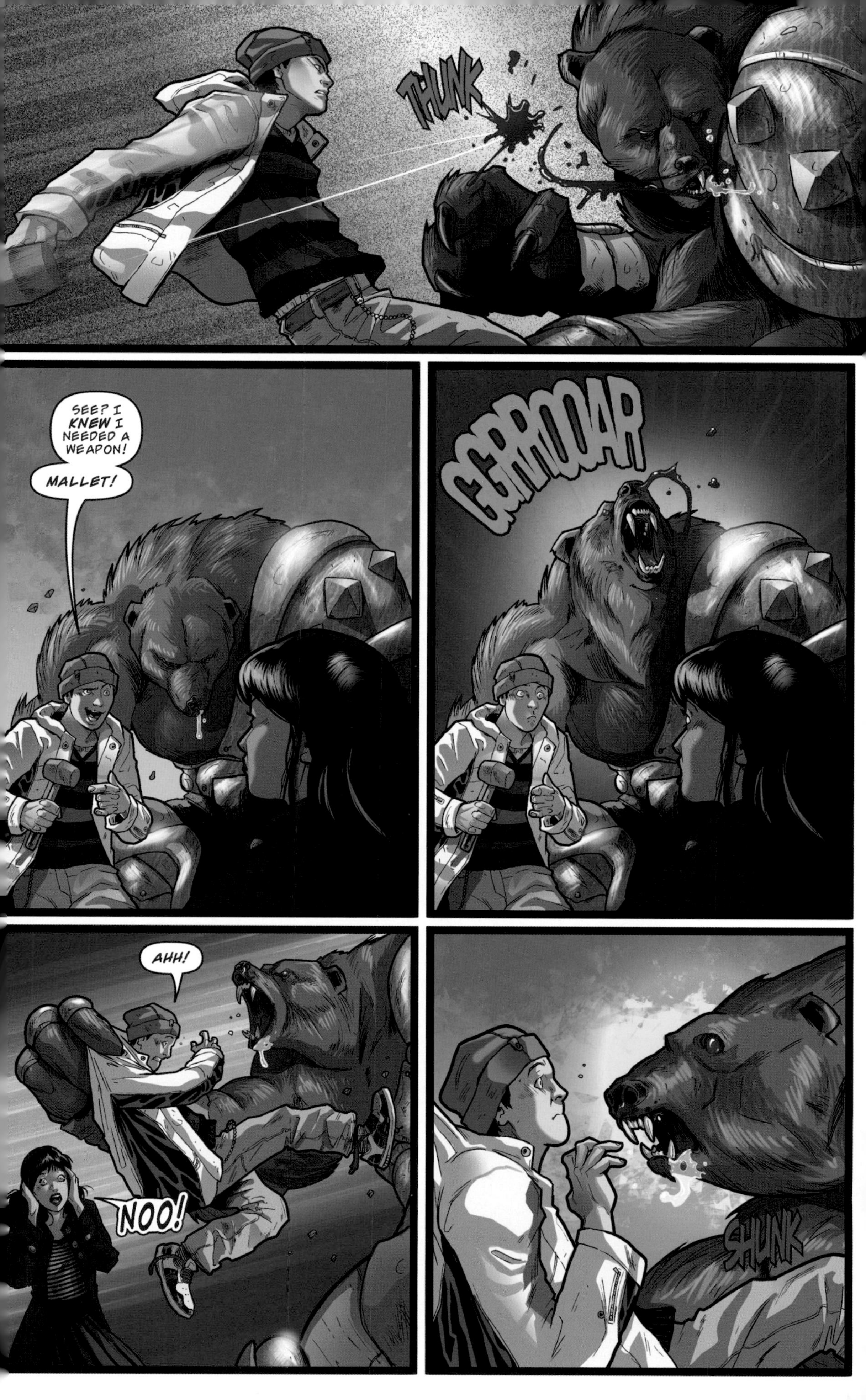
THUNK
SEE? I KNEW I NEEDED A WEAPON!
MALLET!
GGRROOAR
AHH!
NOO!
SHUNK

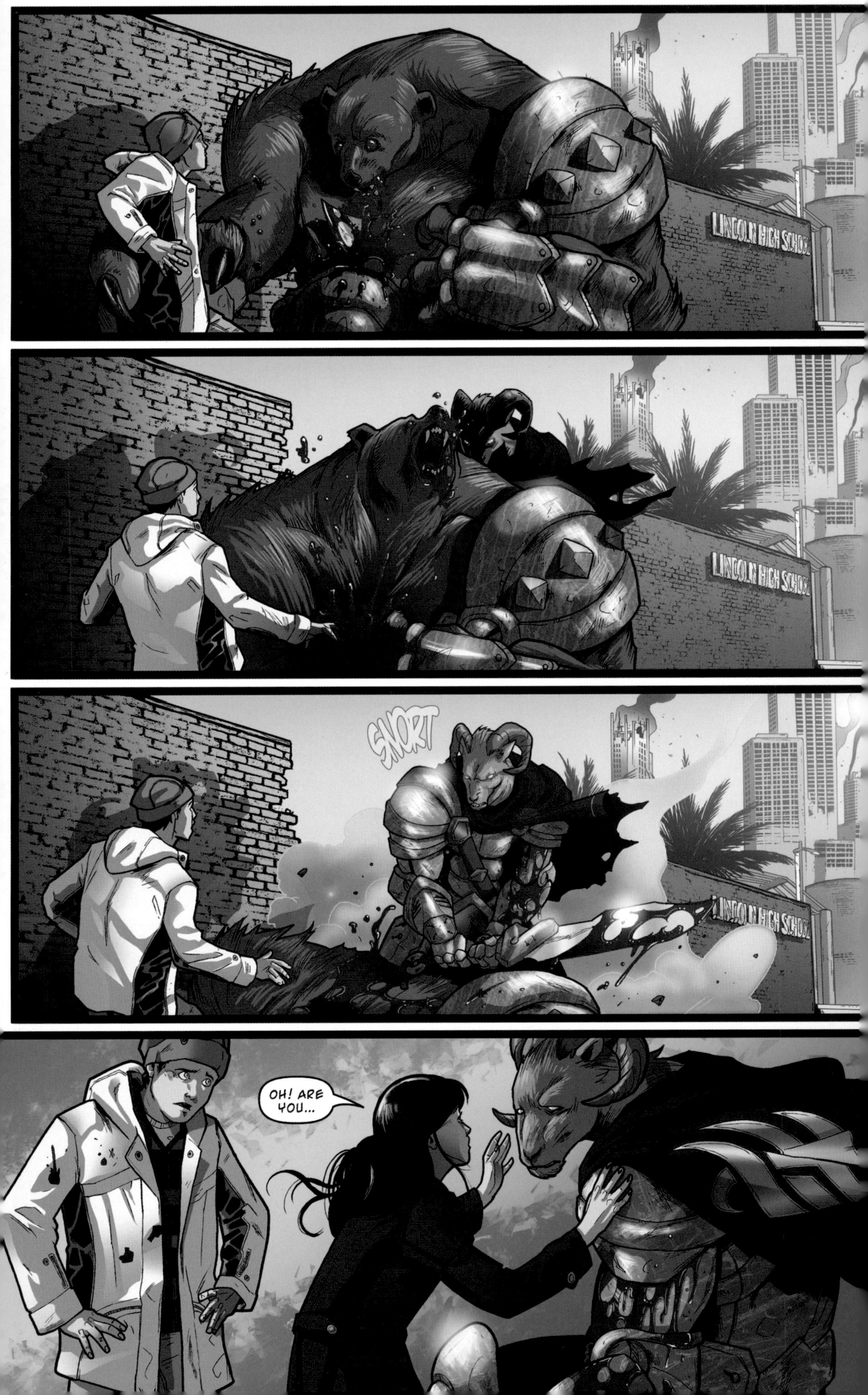
LINCOLN HIGH SCHOOL
LINCOLN HIGH SCHOOL
SNORT
LINCOLN HIGH SCHOOL
OH! ARE YOU...

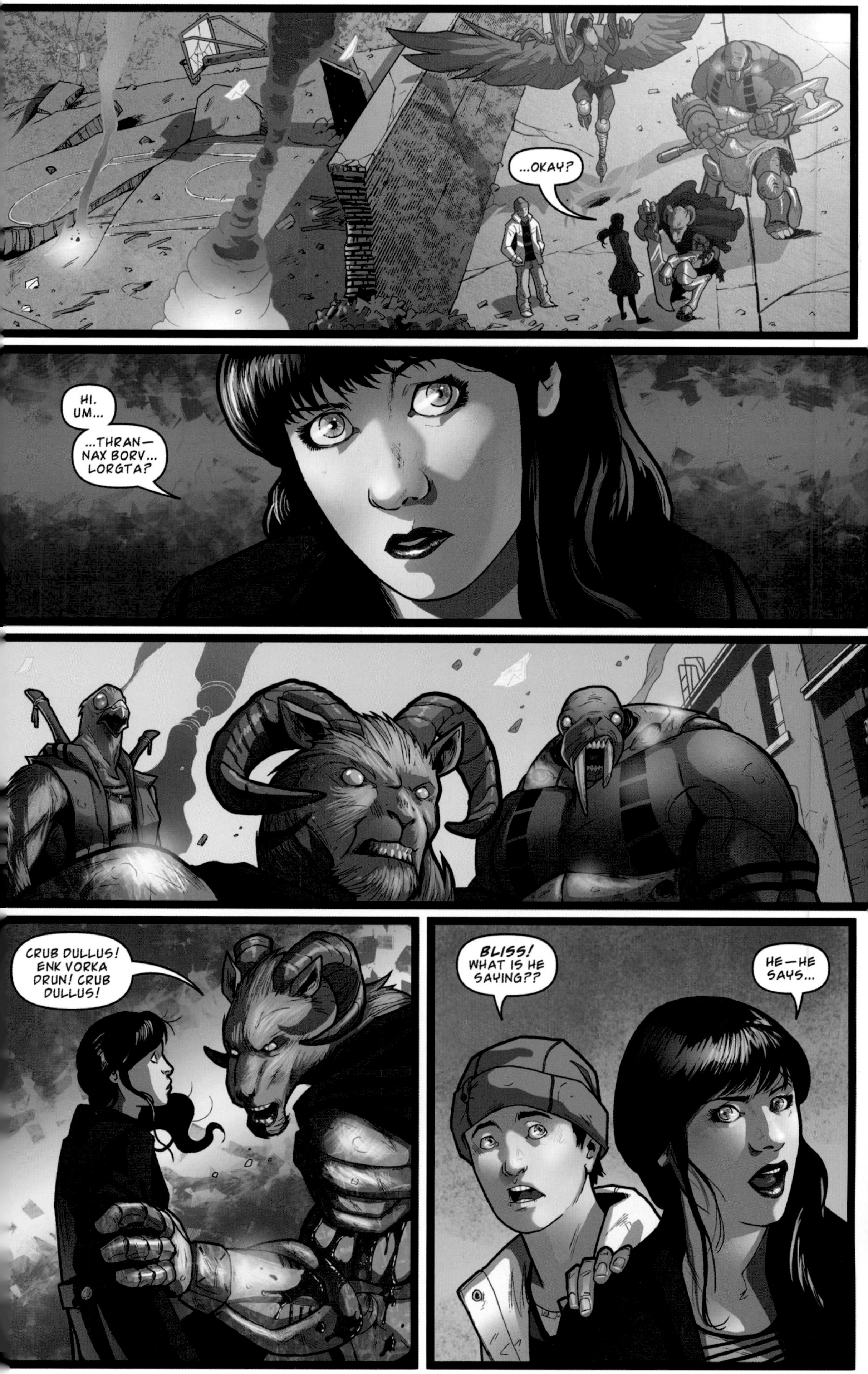
...OKAY?
HI.
UM...
...THRAN—
NAX BORV...
LORGTA?
CRUB DULLUS!
ENK VORKA
DRUN! CRUB
DULLUS!
BLISS!
WHAT IS HE
SAYING??
HE—HE
SAYS...

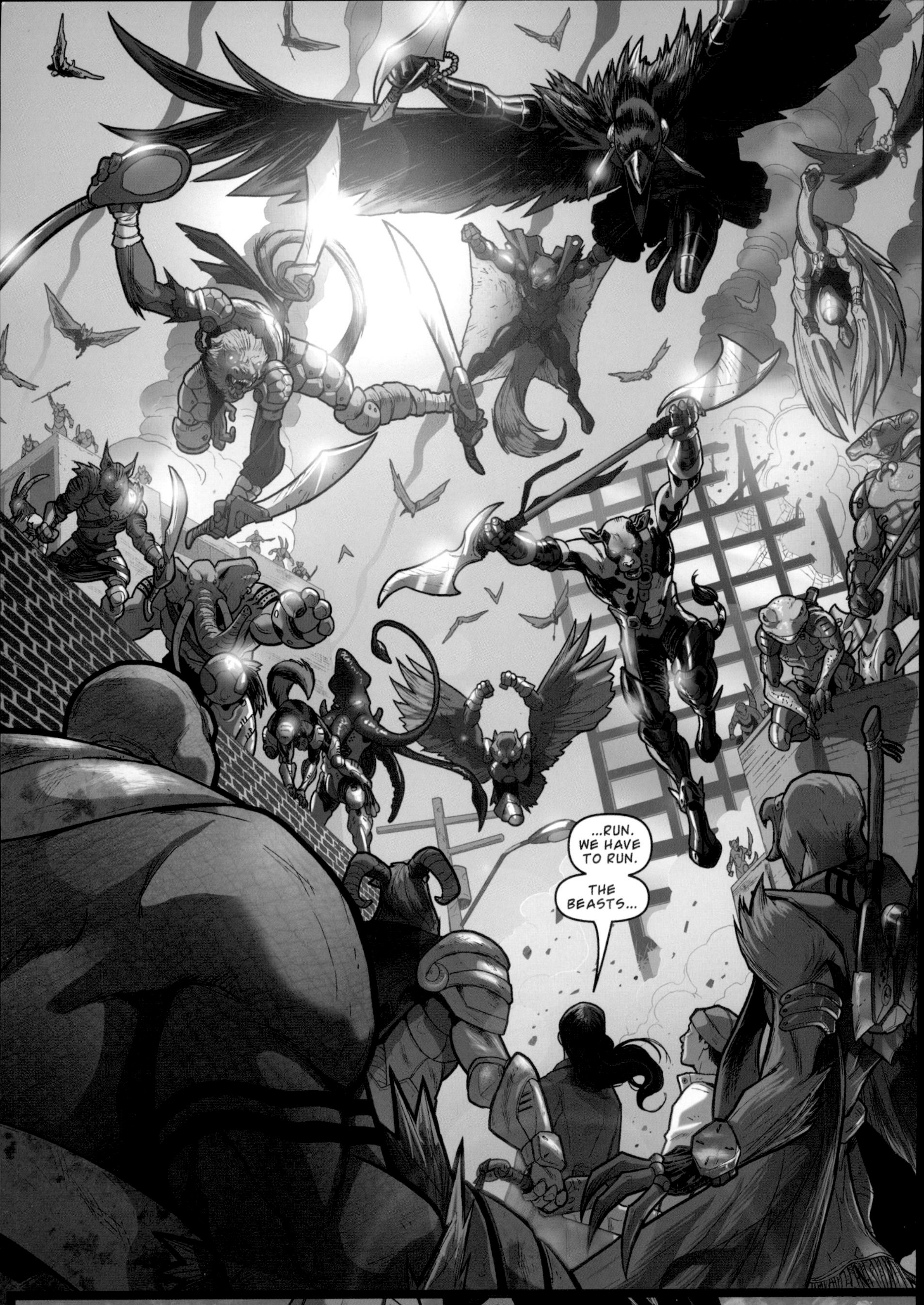
...RUN. WE HAVE TO RUN.
THE BEASTS...

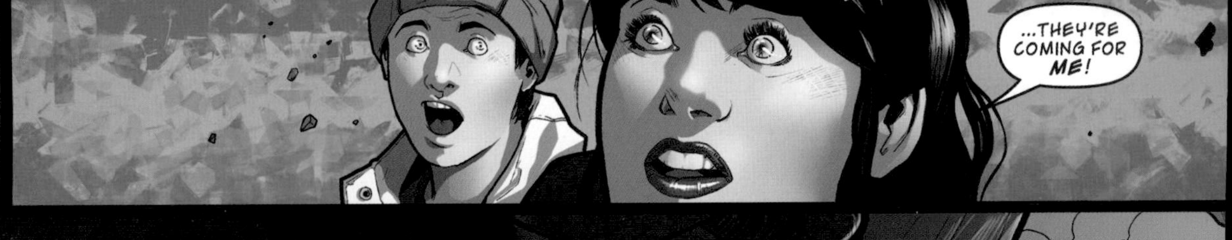
...THEY'RE COMING FOR ME!

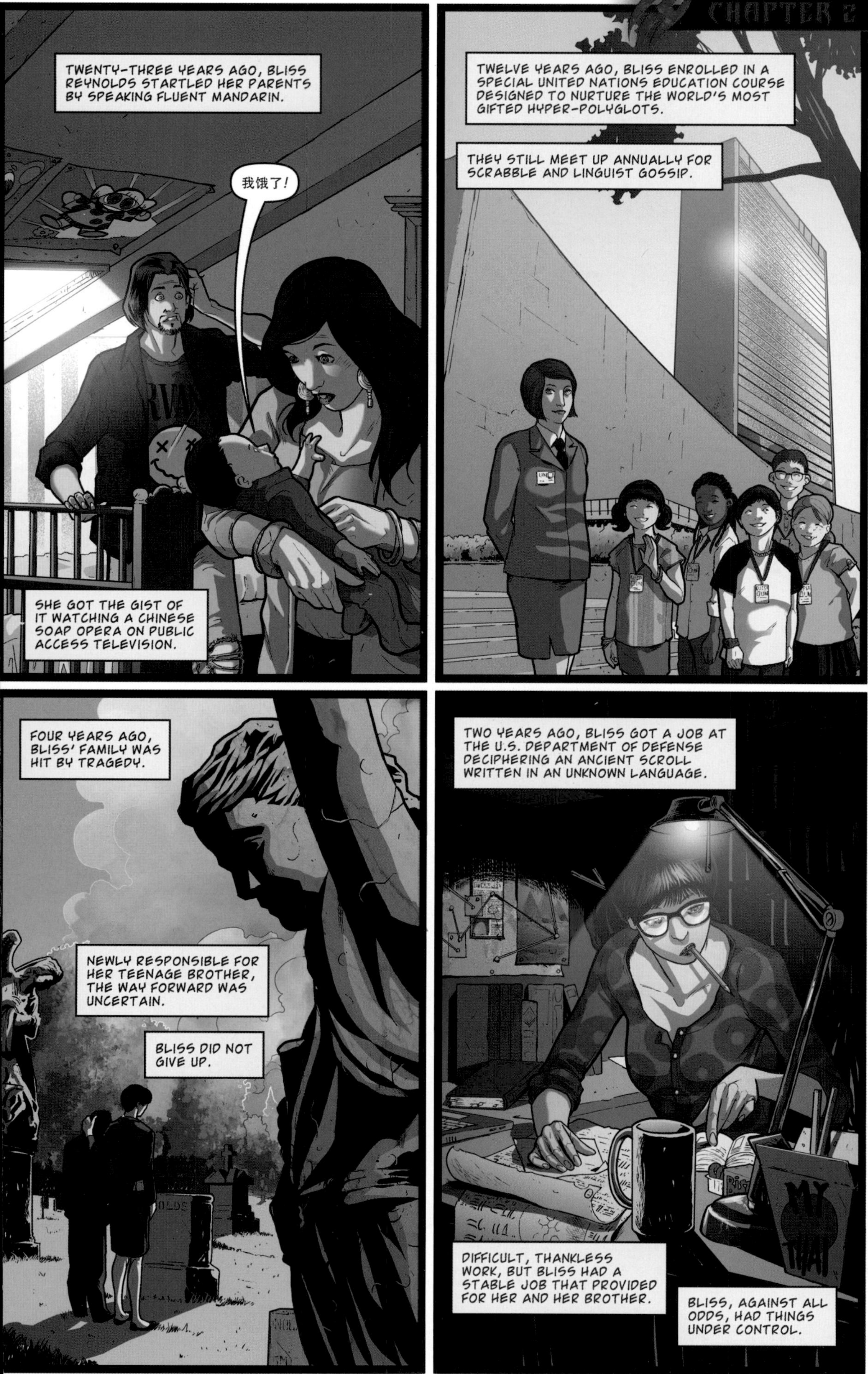
TWENTY-THREE YEARS AGO, BLISS REYNOLDS STARTLED HER PARENTS BY SPEAKING FLUENT MANDARIN.
我饿了!
SHE GOT THE GIST OF IT WATCHING A CHINESE SOAP OPERA ON PUBLIC ACCESS TELEVISION.
TWELVE YEARS AGO, BLISS ENROLLED IN A SPECIAL UNITED NATIONS EDUCATION COURSE DESIGNED TO NURTURE THE WORLD'S MOST GIFTED HYPER-POLYGLOTS.
THEY STILL MEET UP ANNUALLY FOR SCRABBLE AND LINGUIST GOSSIP.
FOUR YEARS AGO, BLISS' FAMILY WAS HIT BY TRAGEDY.
NEWLY RESPONSIBLE FOR HER TEENAGE BROTHER, THE WAY FORWARD WAS UNCERTAIN.
BLISS DID NOT GIVE UP.
TWO YEARS AGO, BLISS GOT A JOB AT THE U.S. DEPARTMENT OF DEFENSE DECIPHERING AN ANCIENT SCROLL WRITTEN IN AN UNKNOWN LANGUAGE.
DIFFICULT, THANKLESS WORK, BUT BLISS HAD A STABLE JOB THAT PROVIDED FOR HER AND HER BROTHER.
BLISS, AGAINST ALL ODDS, HAD THINGS UNDER CONTROL.

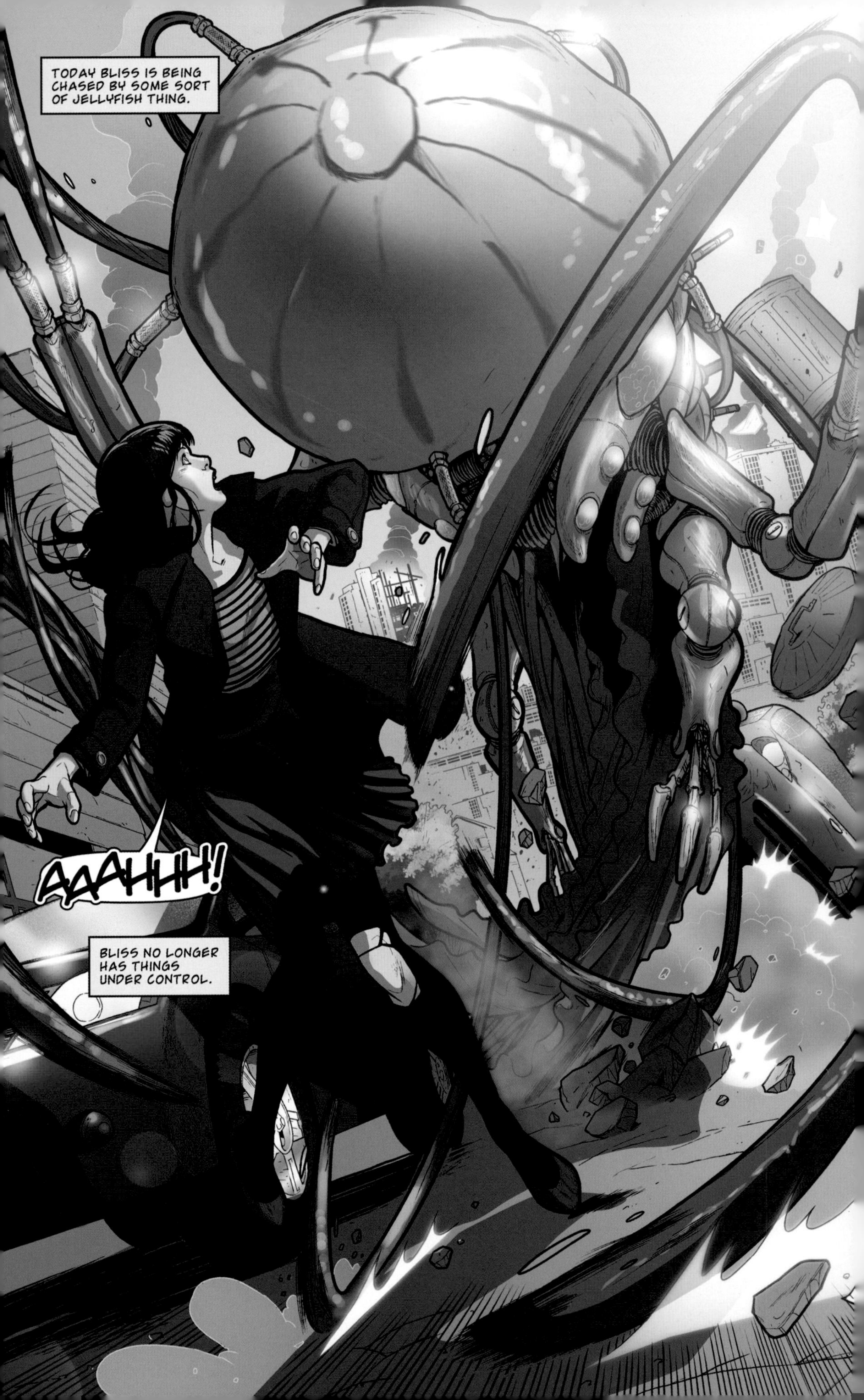
TODAY BLISS IS BEING CHASED BY SOME SORT OF JELLYFISH THING.
AAAHHH!
BLISS NO LONGER HAS THINGS UNDER CONTROL.

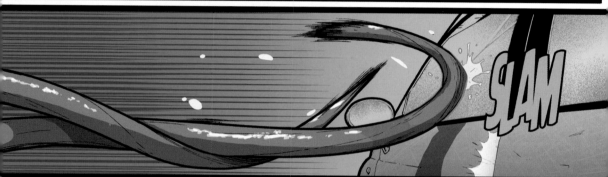

SLAM

GET IT TOGETHER, BLISS. THINK. STOP SCREAMING...

...LIKE A LITTLE GIRL...

HHH!

—ACK!

CRSSH

HA!

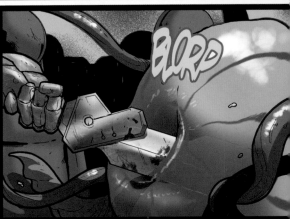

BLORD

I HATE INVERTEBRATES.

THEY'RE NOT SO BAD. ONE OF MY BEST FRIENDS WAS AN INVERTEBRATE.

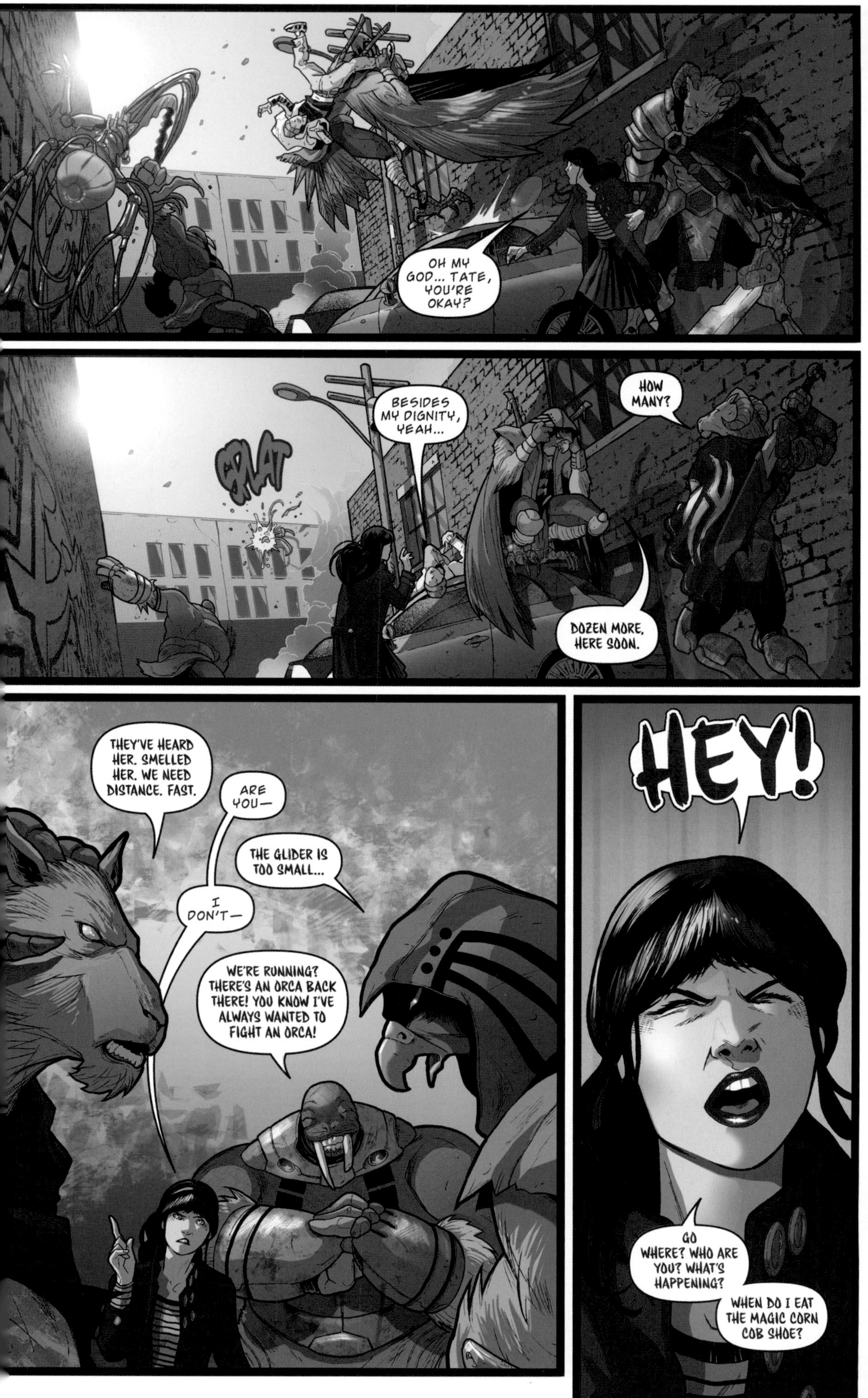
OH MY GOD... TATE, YOU'RE OKAY?
BESIDES MY DIGNITY, YEAH...
HOW MANY?
DOZEN MORE, HERE SOON.
GLAT
THEY'VE HEARD HER. SMELLED HER. WE NEED DISTANCE. FAST.
ARE YOU—
THE GLIDER IS TOO SMALL...
I DON'T—
WE'RE RUNNING? THERE'S AN ORCA BACK THERE! YOU KNOW I'VE ALWAYS WANTED TO FIGHT AN ORCA!
HEY!
GO WHERE? WHO ARE YOU? WHAT'S HAPPENING?
WHEN DO I EAT THE MAGIC CORN COB SHOE?

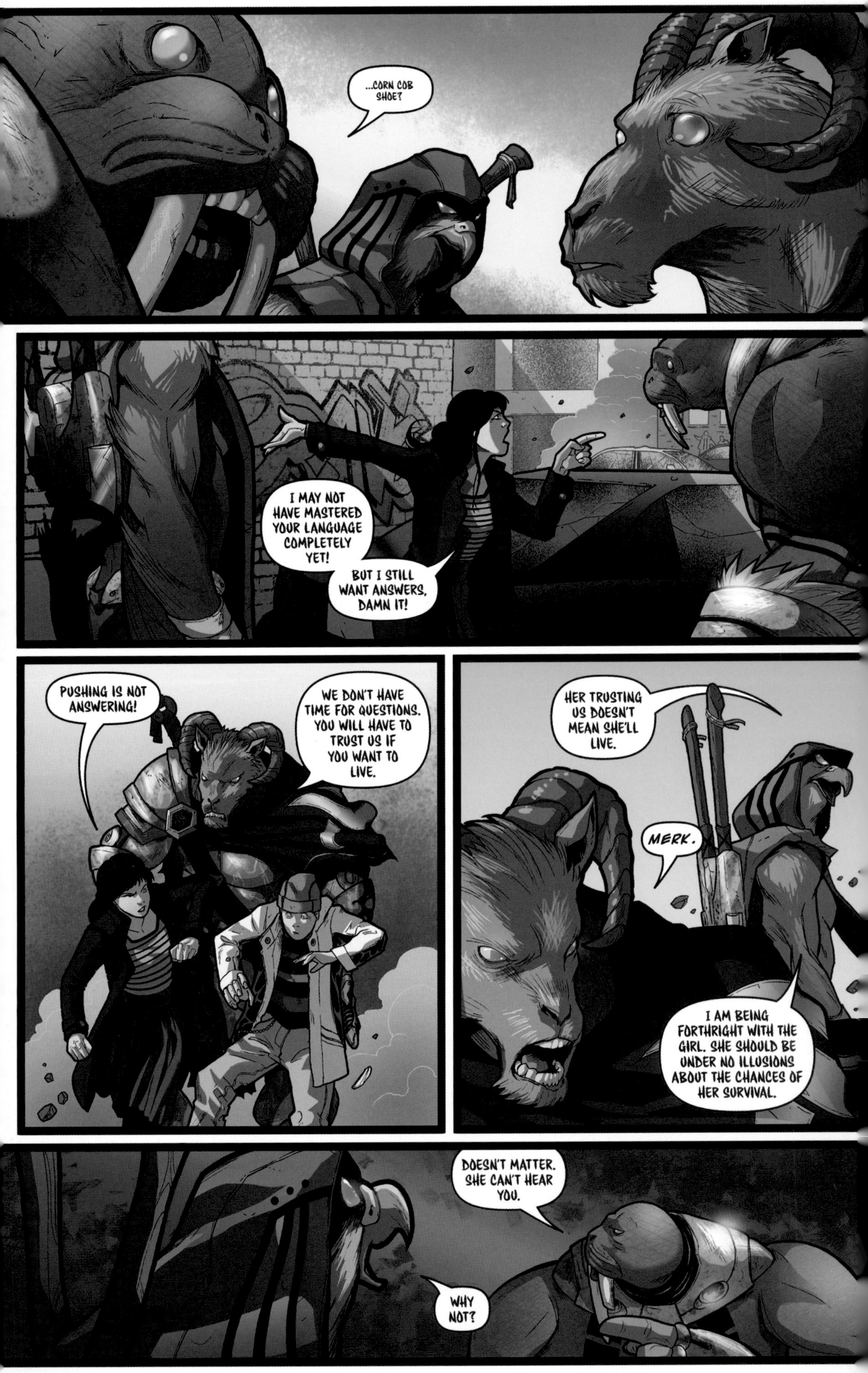
...CORN COB SHOE?
I MAY NOT HAVE MASTERED YOUR LANGUAGE COMPLETELY YET!
BUT I STILL WANT ANSWERS, DAMN IT!
PUSHING IS NOT ANSWERING!
WE DON'T HAVE TIME FOR QUESTIONS. YOU WILL HAVE TO TRUST US IF YOU WANT TO LIVE.
HER TRUSTING US DOESN'T MEAN SHE'LL LIVE.
MERK.
I AM BEING FORTHRIGHT WITH THE GIRL. SHE SHOULD BE UNDER NO ILLUSIONS ABOUT THE CHANCES OF HER SURVIVAL.
DOESN'T MATTER. SHE CAN'T HEAR YOU.
WHY NOT?

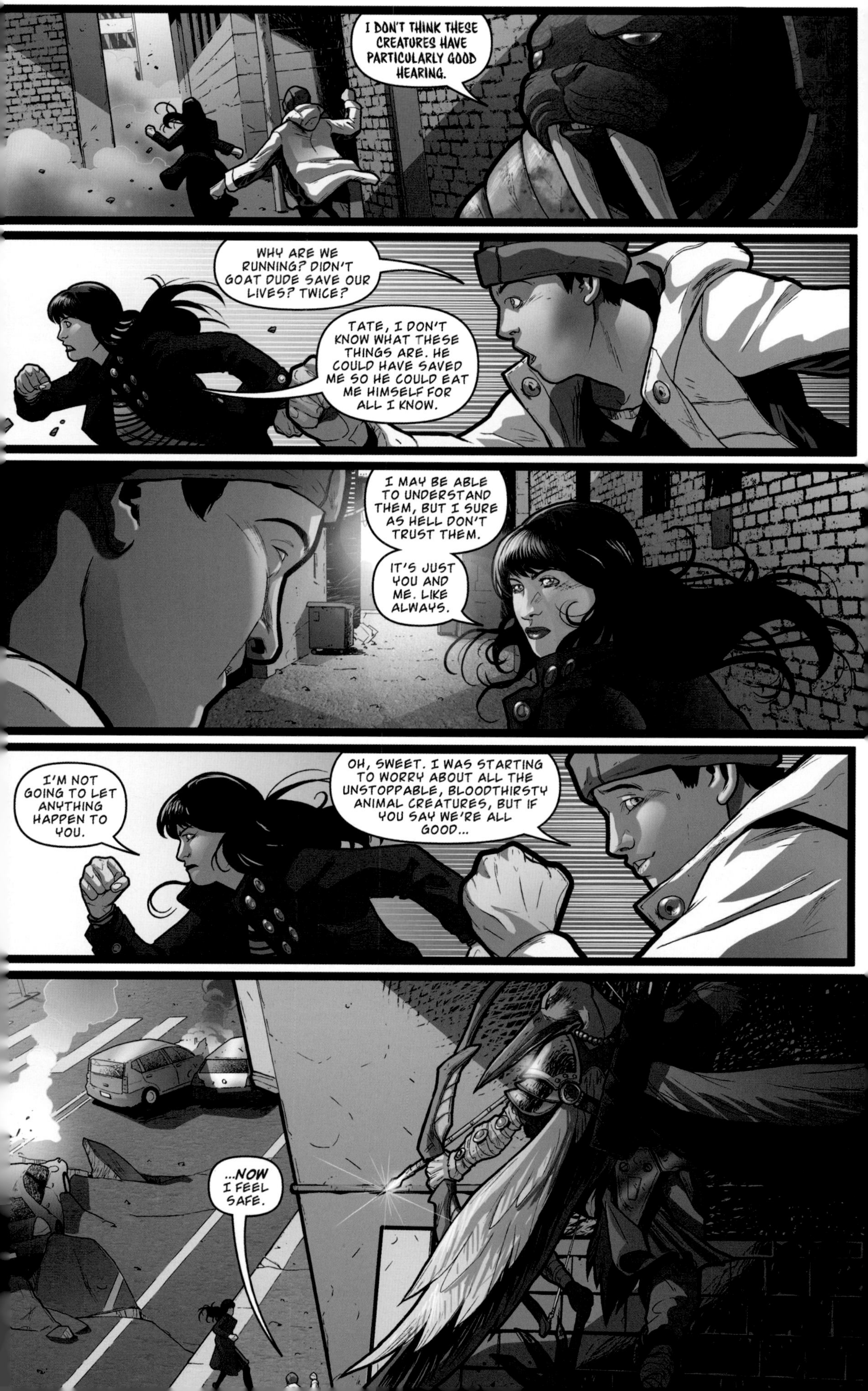
I DON'T THINK THESE CREATURES HAVE PARTICULARLY GOOD HEARING.
WHY ARE WE RUNNING? DIDN'T GOAT DUDE SAVE OUR LIVES? TWICE?
TATE, I DON'T KNOW WHAT THESE THINGS ARE. HE COULD HAVE SAVED ME SO HE COULD EAT ME HIMSELF FOR ALL I KNOW.
I MAY BE ABLE TO UNDERSTAND THEM, BUT I SURE AS HELL DON'T TRUST THEM.
IT'S JUST YOU AND ME. LIKE ALWAYS.
I'M NOT GOING TO LET ANYTHING HAPPEN TO YOU.
OH, SWEET. I WAS STARTING TO WORRY ABOUT ALL THE UNSTOPPABLE, BLOODTHIRSTY ANIMAL CREATURES, BUT IF YOU SAY WE'RE ALL GOOD...
...NOW I FEEL SAFE.

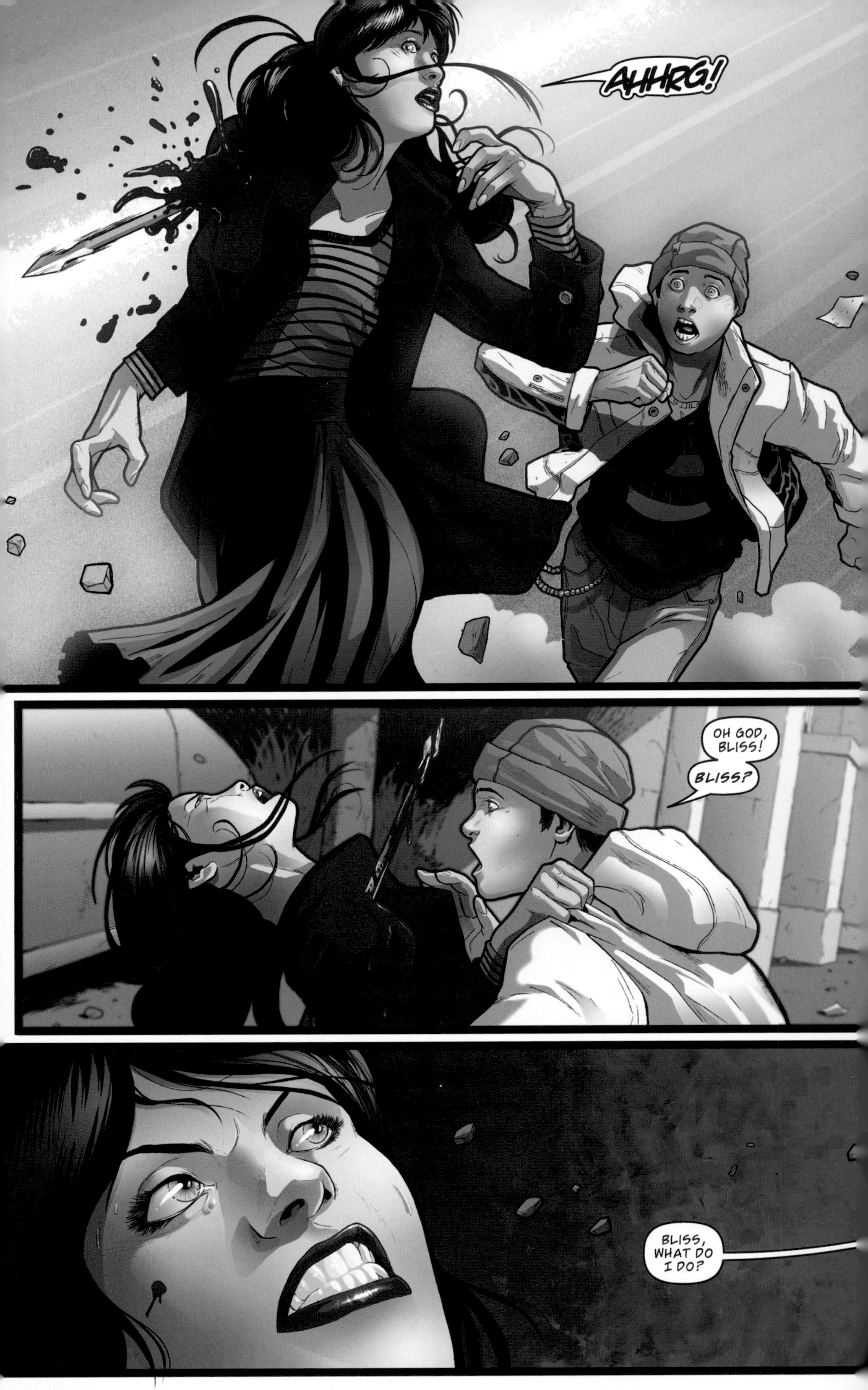
AHHRG!
OH GOD, BLISS!
BLISS?
BLISS, WHAT DO I DO?

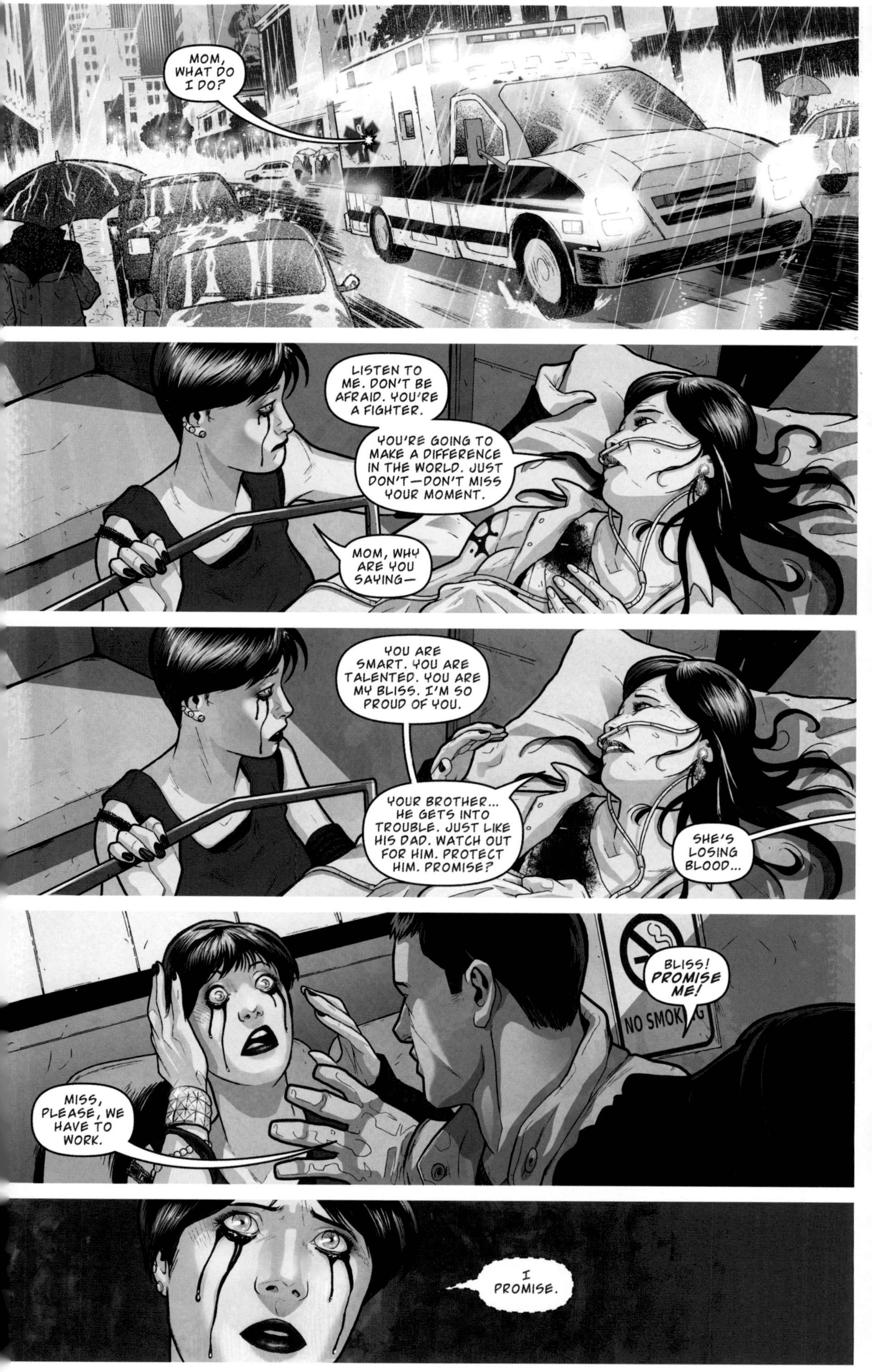
MOM, WHAT DO I DO?
LISTEN TO ME. DON'T BE AFRAID. YOU'RE A FIGHTER.
YOU'RE GOING TO MAKE A DIFFERENCE IN THE WORLD. JUST DON'T—DON'T MISS YOUR MOMENT.
MOM, WHY ARE YOU SAYING—
YOU ARE SMART. YOU ARE TALENTED. YOU ARE MY BLISS. I'M SO PROUD OF YOU.
YOUR BROTHER... HE GETS INTO TROUBLE. JUST LIKE HIS DAD. WATCH OUT FOR HIM. PROTECT HIM. PROMISE?
SHE'S LOSING BLOOD...
BLISS! PROMISE ME!
NO SMOK
MISS, PLEASE, WE HAVE TO WORK.
I PROMISE.

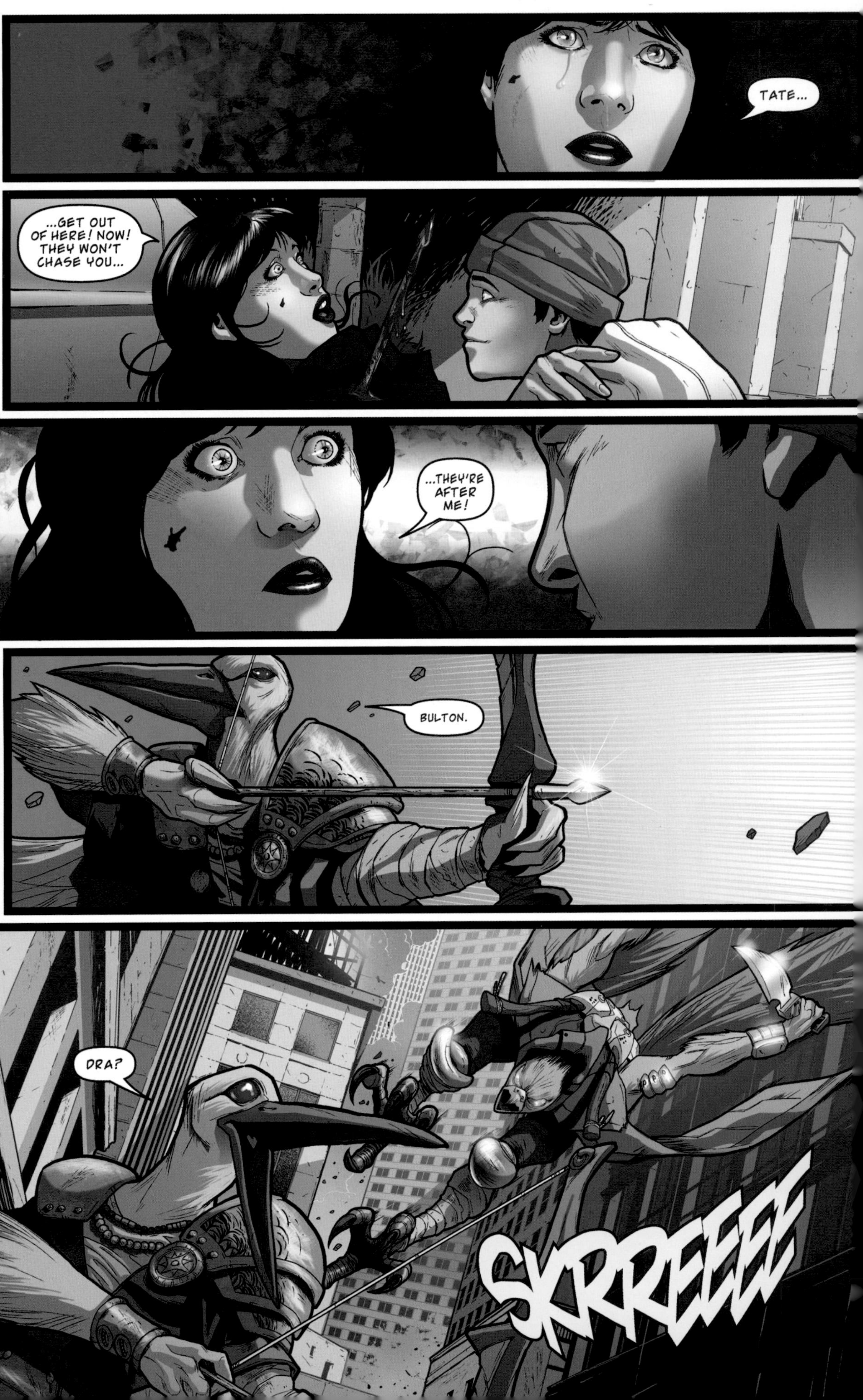
TATE...
...GET OUT OF HERE! NOW! THEY WON'T CHASE YOU...
...THEY'RE AFTER ME!
BULTON.
DRA?
SKREEEE

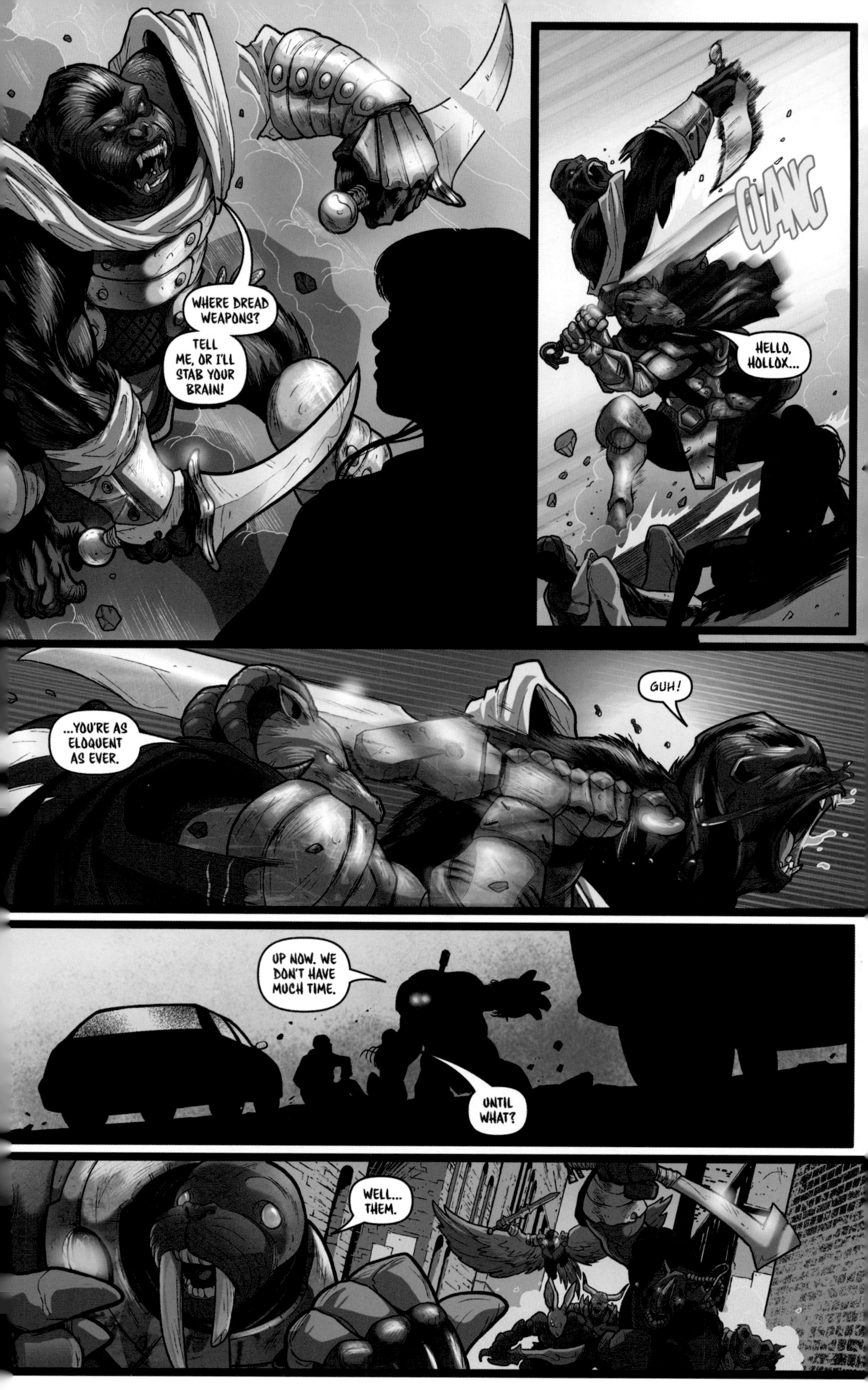
WHERE DREAD WEAPONS?
TELL ME, OR I'LL STAB YOUR BRAIN!
CLANG
HELLO, HOLLOX...
...YOU'RE AS ELOQUENT AS EVER.
GUH!
UP NOW. WE DON'T HAVE MUCH TIME.
UNTIL WHAT?
WELL... THEM.

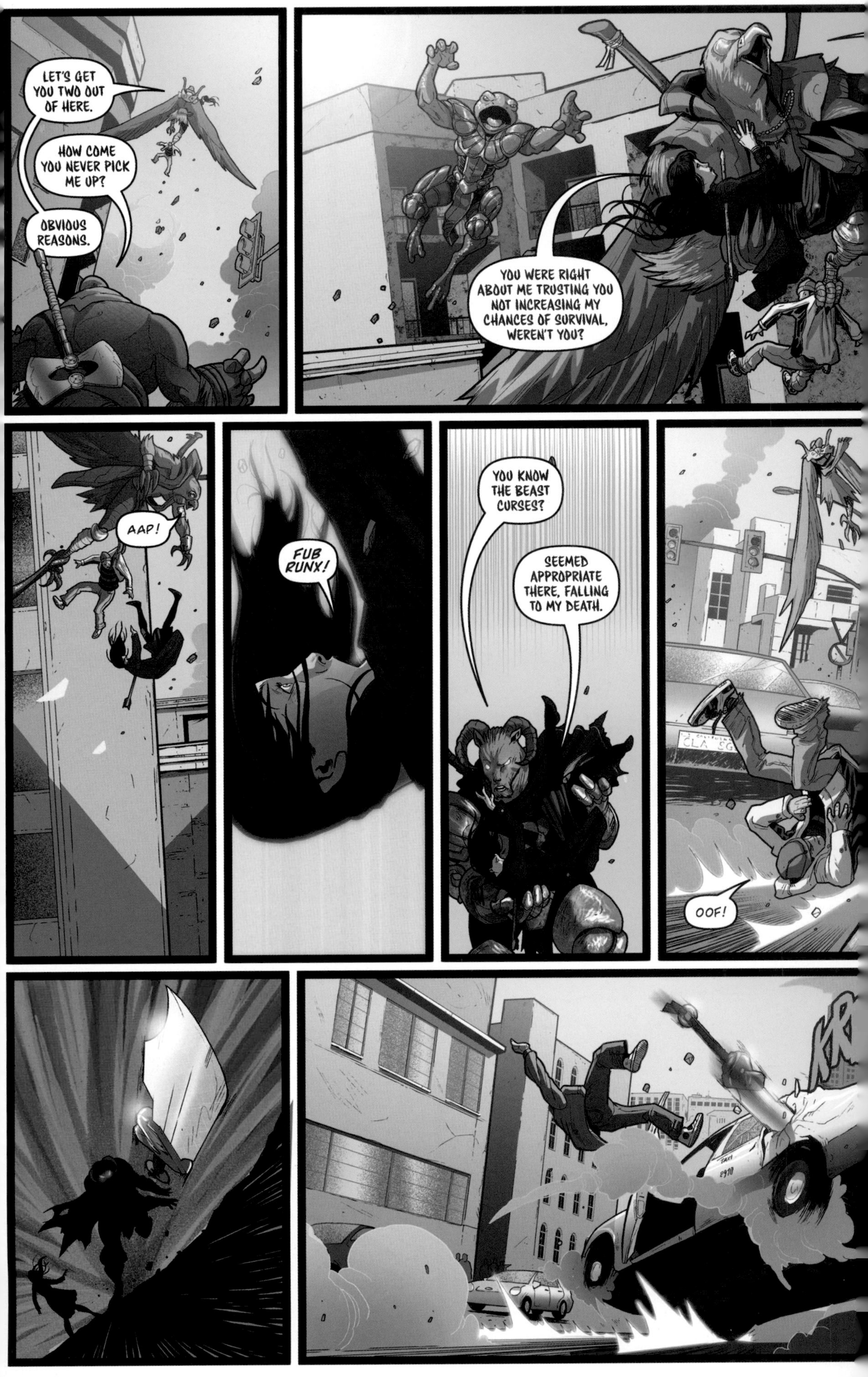
LET'S GET YOU TWO OUT OF HERE.
HOW COME YOU NEVER PICK ME UP?
OBVIOUS REASONS.
YOU WERE RIGHT ABOUT ME TRUSTING YOU NOT INCREASING MY CHANCES OF SURVIVAL, WEREN'T YOU?
AAP!
FUB RUNX!
YOU KNOW THE BEAST CURSES?
SEEMED APPROPRIATE THERE, FALLING TO MY DEATH.
OOF!

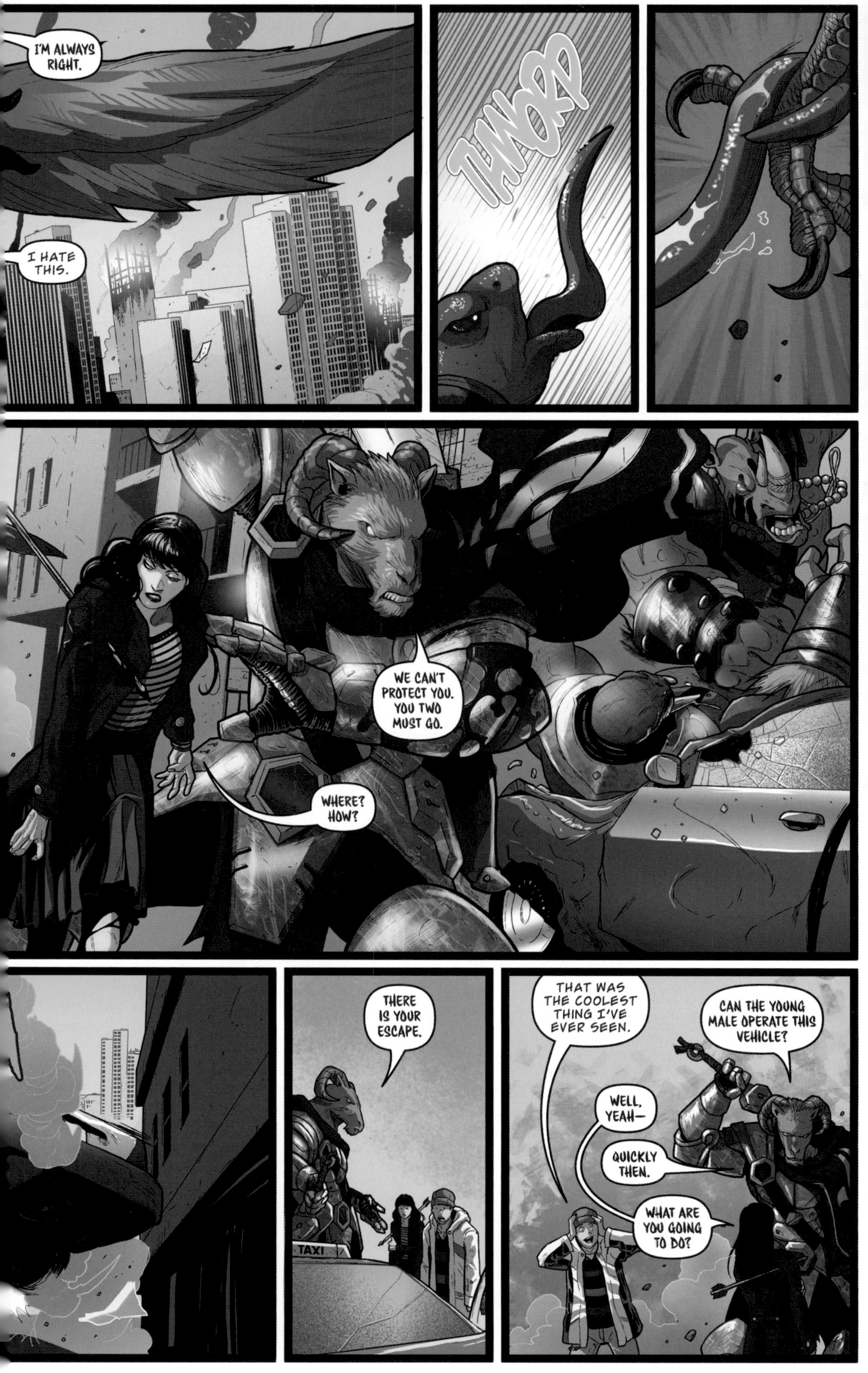
I'M ALWAYS RIGHT.
I HATE THIS.
THWORP
WE CAN'T PROTECT YOU. YOU TWO MUST GO.
WHERE? HOW?
THERE IS YOUR ESCAPE.
TAXI
THAT WAS THE COOLEST THING I'VE EVER SEEN.
CAN THE YOUNG MALE OPERATE THIS VEHICLE?
WELL, YEAH—
QUICKLY THEN.
WHAT ARE YOU GOING TO DO?

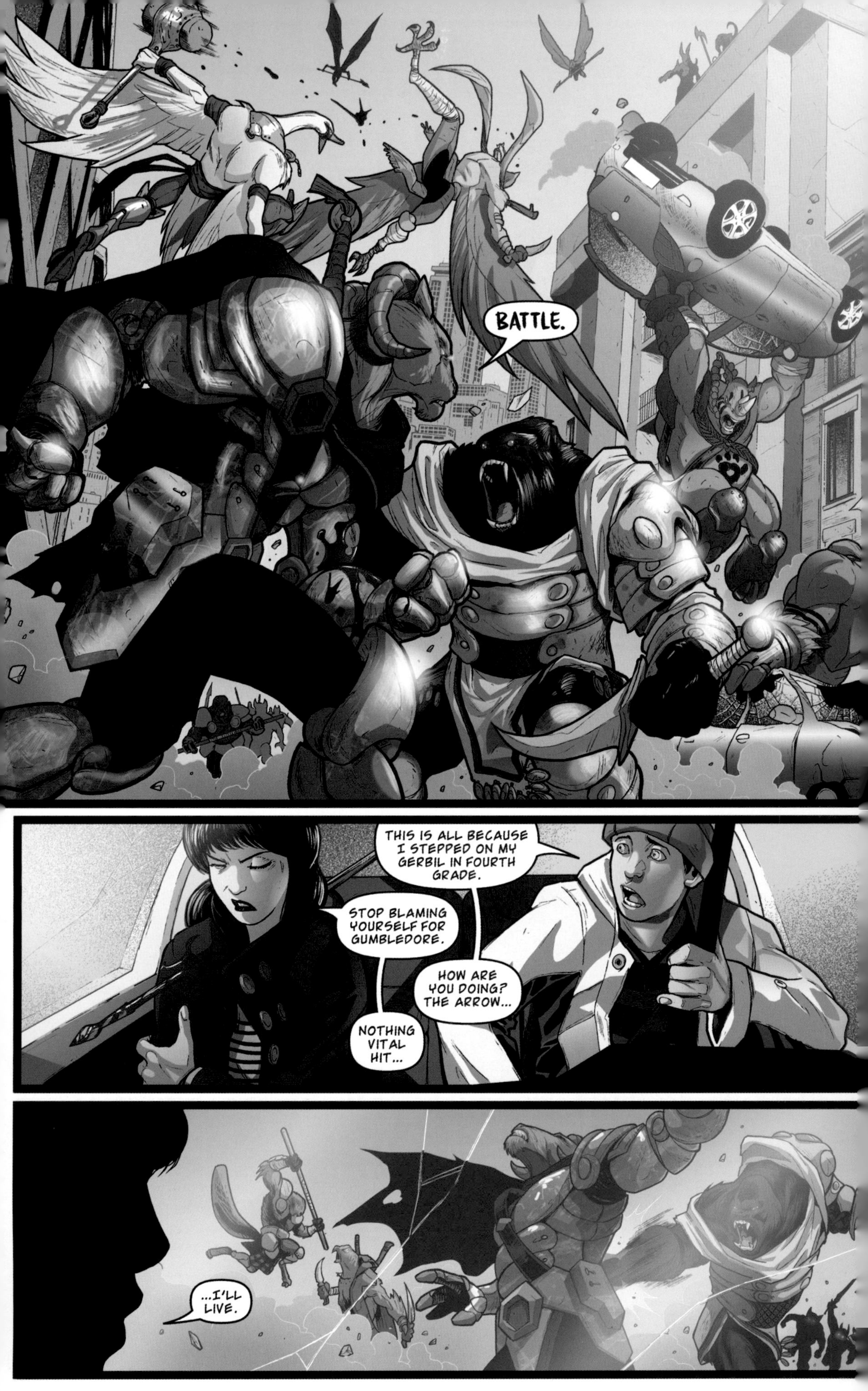
BATTLE.
THIS IS ALL BECAUSE I STEPPED ON MY GERBIL IN FOURTH GRADE.
STOP BLAMING YOURSELF FOR GUMBLEDORE.
HOW ARE YOU DOING? THE ARROW...
NOTHING VITAL HIT...
...I'LL LIVE.

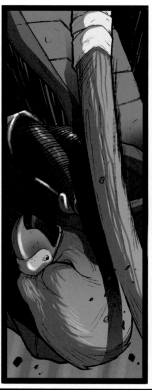

SHALL WE ACT?

MM. NOT YET. I'M HAVING FAR TOO MUCH FUN WATCHING.

DEATH TO THE TRAITOR!

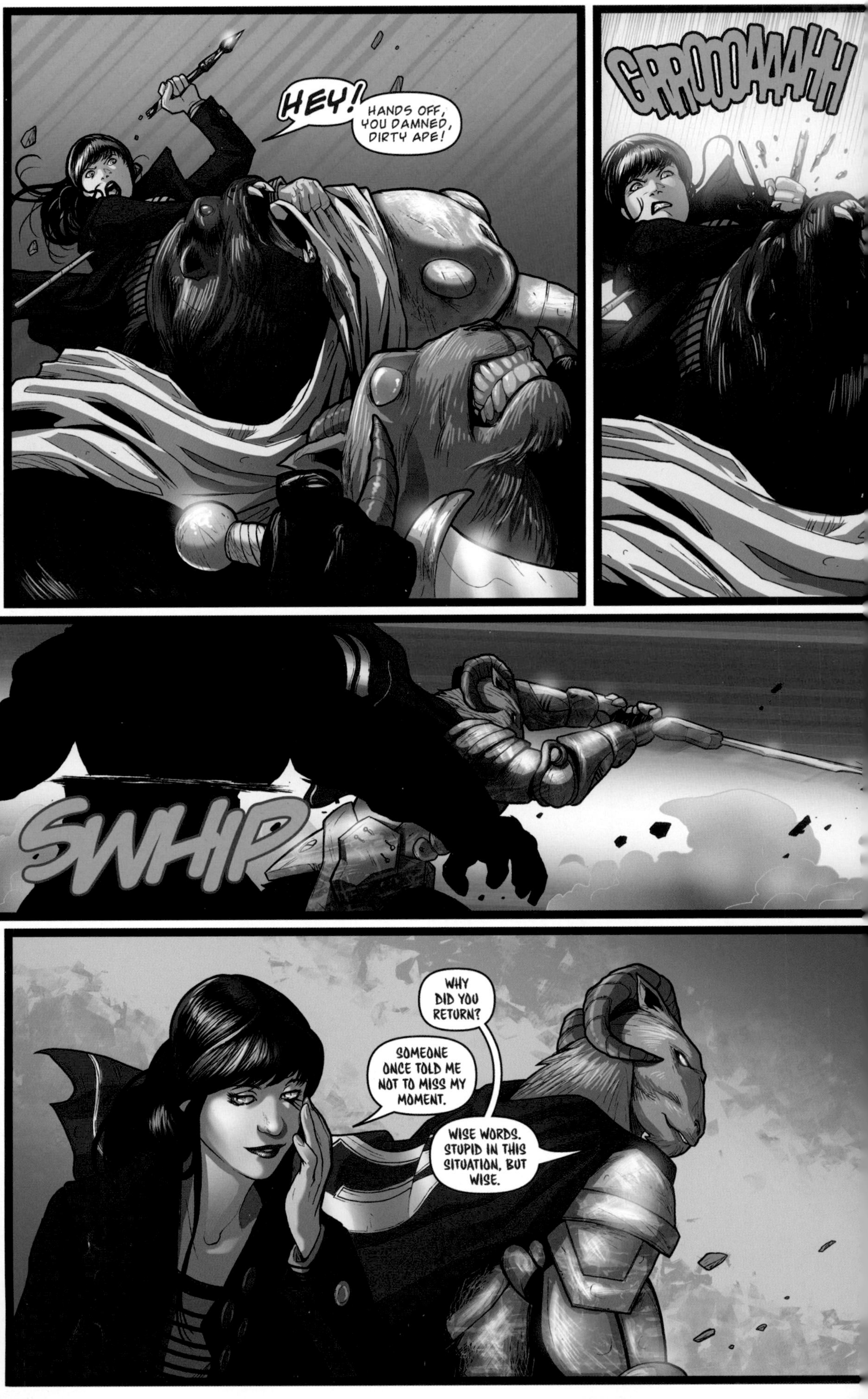
HEY!
HANDS OFF, YOU DAMNED, DIRTY APE!
GRROOOAAAHH
SWHIP
WHY DID YOU RETURN?
SOMEONE ONCE TOLD ME NOT TO MISS MY MOMENT.
WISE WORDS. STUPID IN THIS SITUATION, BUT WISE.

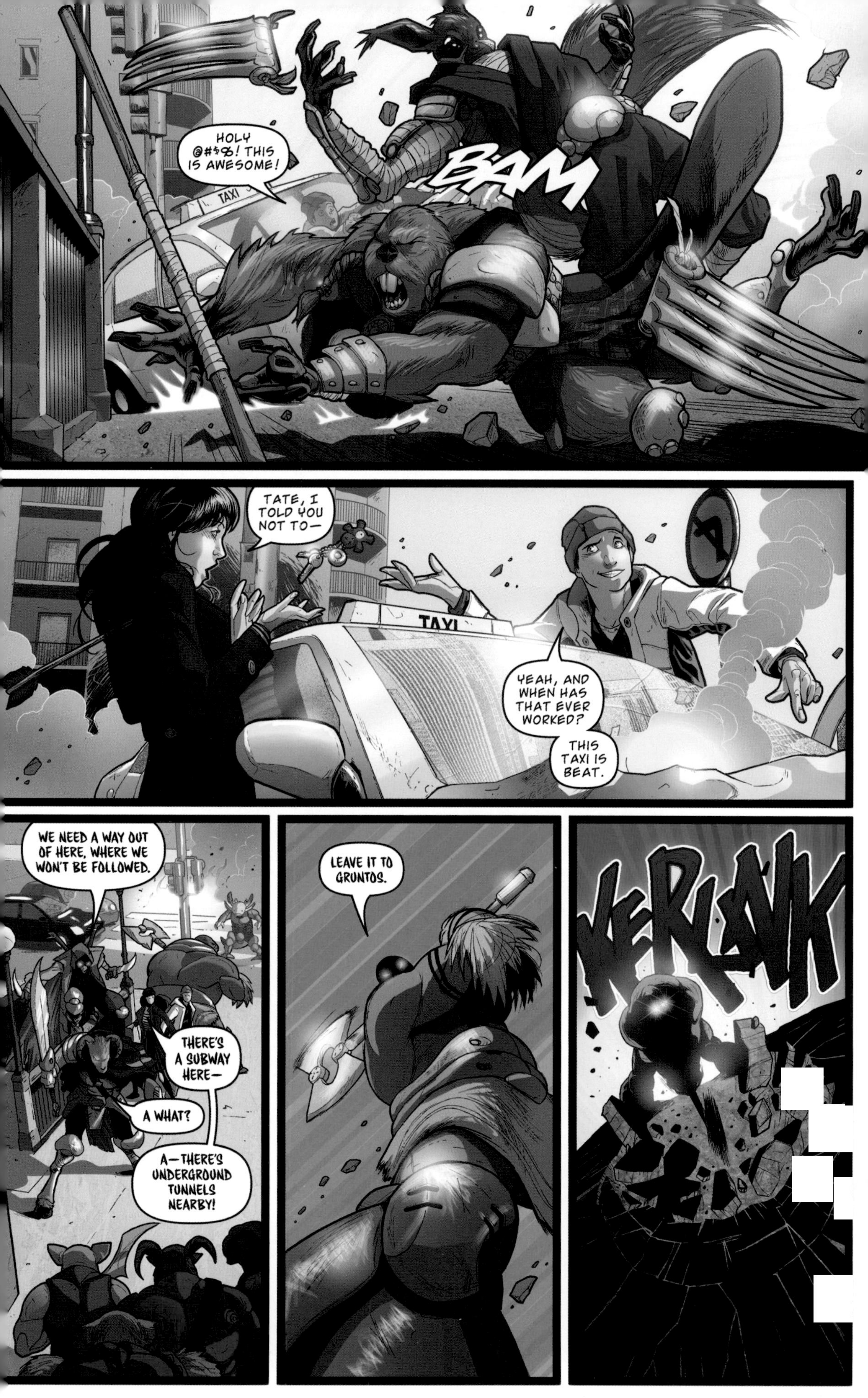
HOLY @#$%! THIS IS AWESOME!
TAXI
BAM
TATE, I TOLD YOU NOT TO—
TAXI
YEAH, AND WHEN HAS THAT EVER WORKED?
THIS TAXI IS BEAT.
WE NEED A WAY OUT OF HERE, WHERE WE WON'T BE FOLLOWED.
THERE'S A SUBWAY HERE—
A WHAT?
A—THERE'S UNDERGROUND TUNNELS NEARBY!
LEAVE IT TO GRUNTOS.
KERLANK

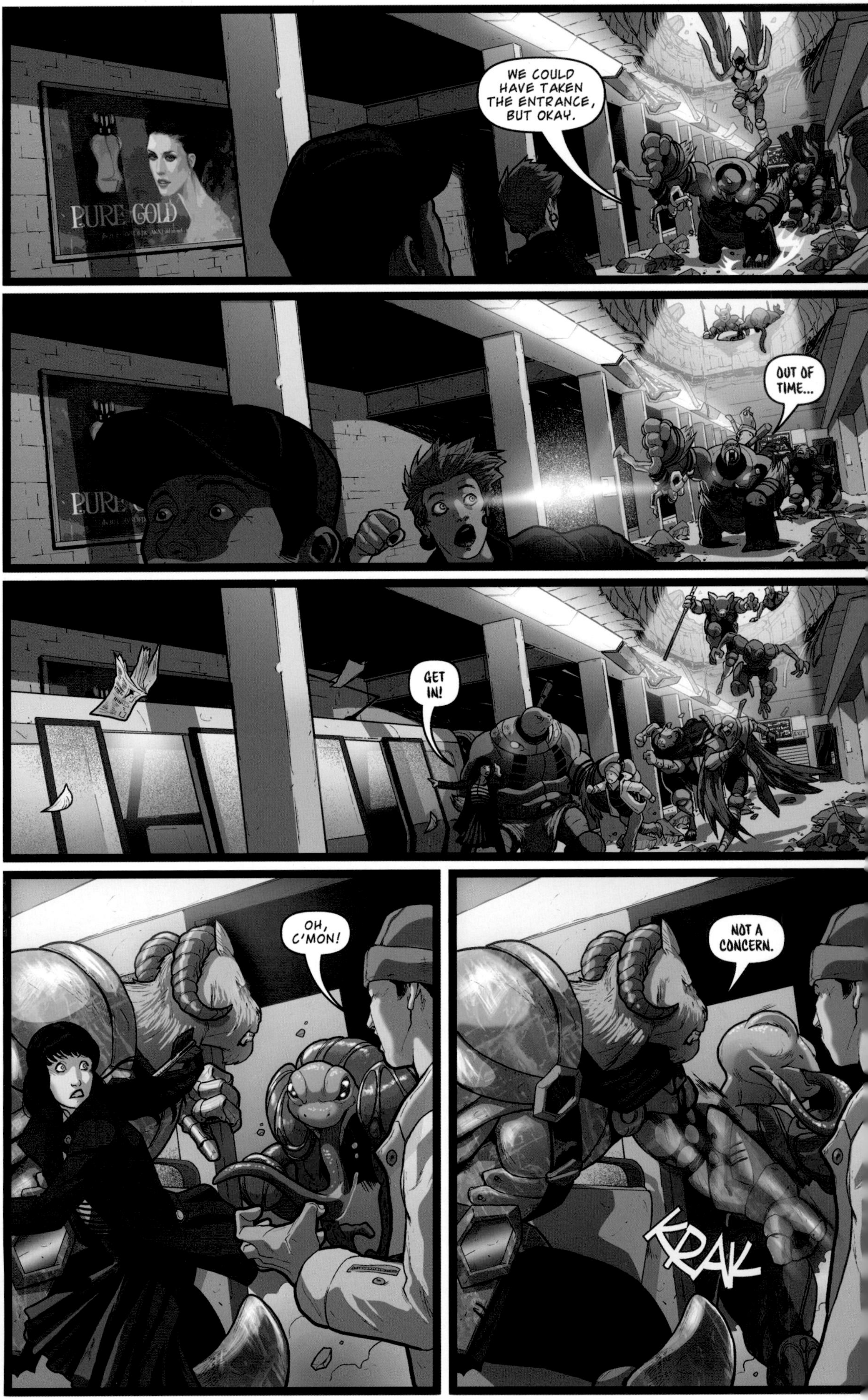
PURE GOLD
WE COULD HAVE TAKEN THE ENTRANCE, BUT OKAY.
OUT OF TIME...
GET IN!
OH, C'MON!
NOT A CONCERN.
KRAK

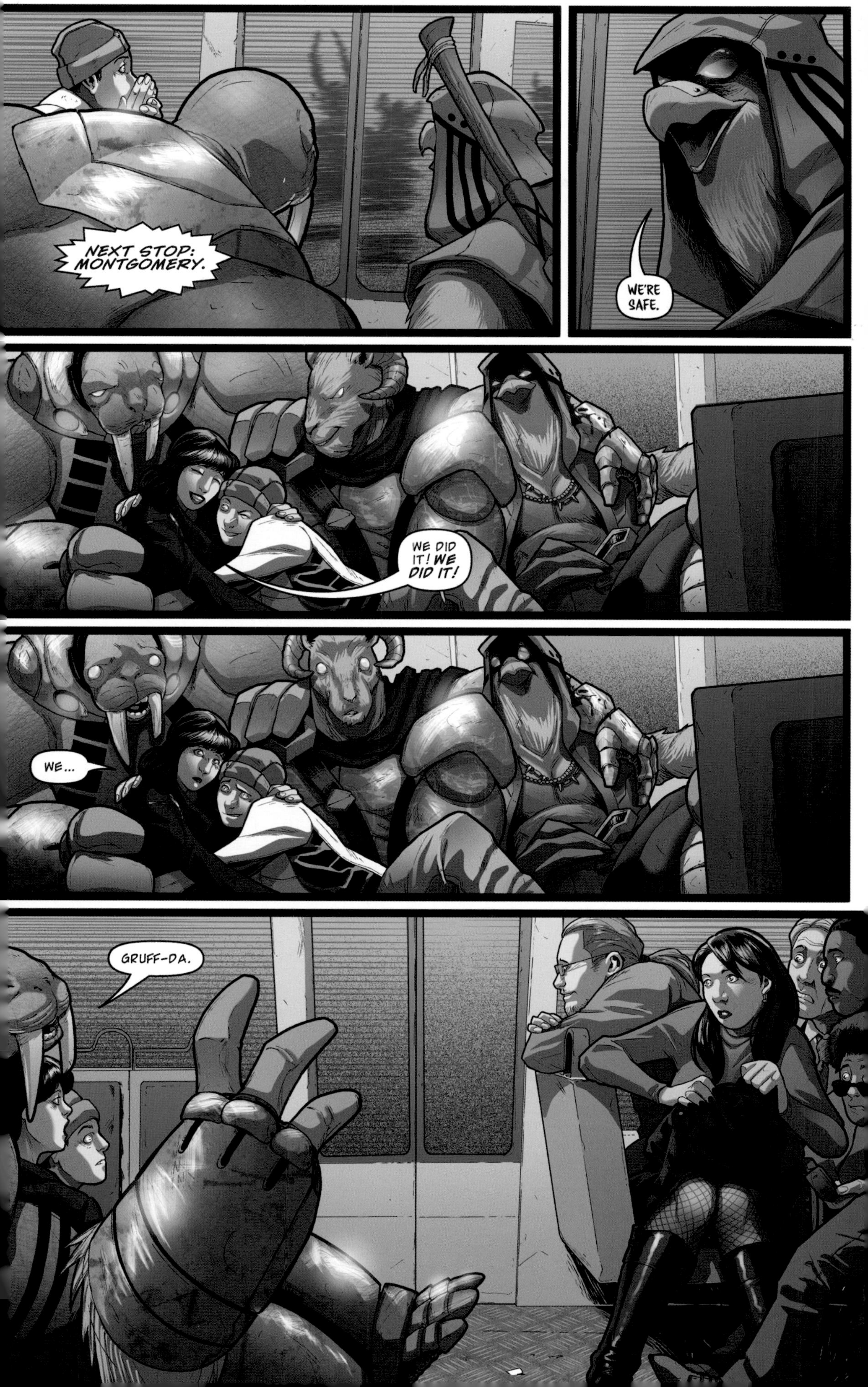
NEXT STOP: MONTGOMERY.
WE'RE SAFE.
WE DID IT! WE DID IT!
WE...
GRUFF-DA.

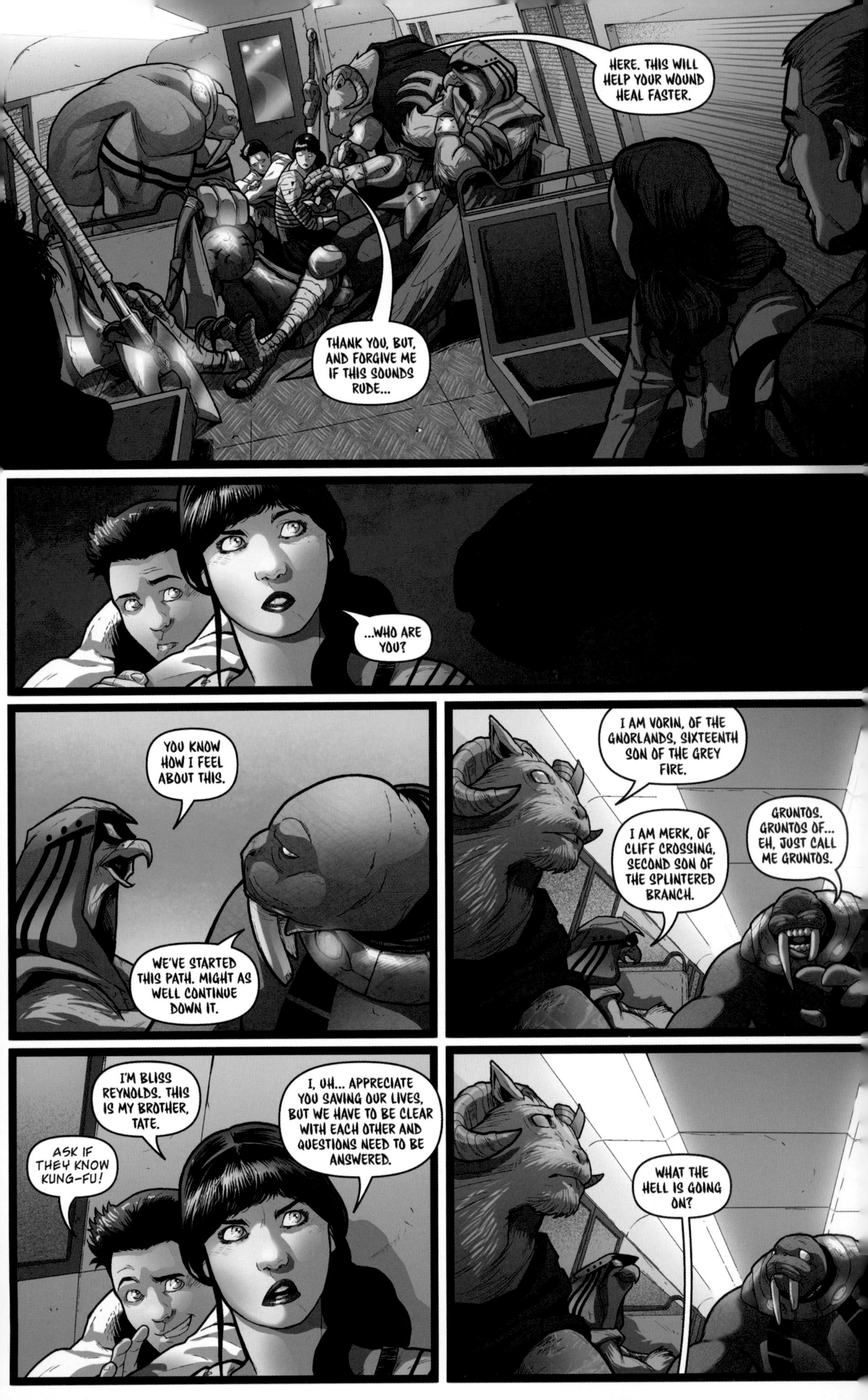
HERE. THIS WILL HELP YOUR WOUND HEAL FASTER.
THANK YOU, BUT, AND FORGIVE ME IF THIS SOUNDS RUDE...
...WHO ARE YOU?
YOU KNOW HOW I FEEL ABOUT THIS.
WE'VE STARTED THIS PATH. MIGHT AS WELL CONTINUE DOWN IT.
I AM VORIN, OF THE GNORLANDS, SIXTEENTH SON OF THE GREY FIRE.
I AM MERK, OF CLIFF CROSSING, SECOND SON OF THE SPLINTERED BRANCH.
GRUNTOS. GRUNTOS OF... EH, JUST CALL ME GRUNTOS.
I'M BLISS REYNOLDS. THIS IS MY BROTHER, TATE.
ASK IF THEY KNOW KUNG-FU!
I, UH... APPRECIATE YOU SAVING OUR LIVES, BUT WE HAVE TO BE CLEAR WITH EACH OTHER AND QUESTIONS NEED TO BE ANSWERED.
WHAT THE HELL IS GOING ON?

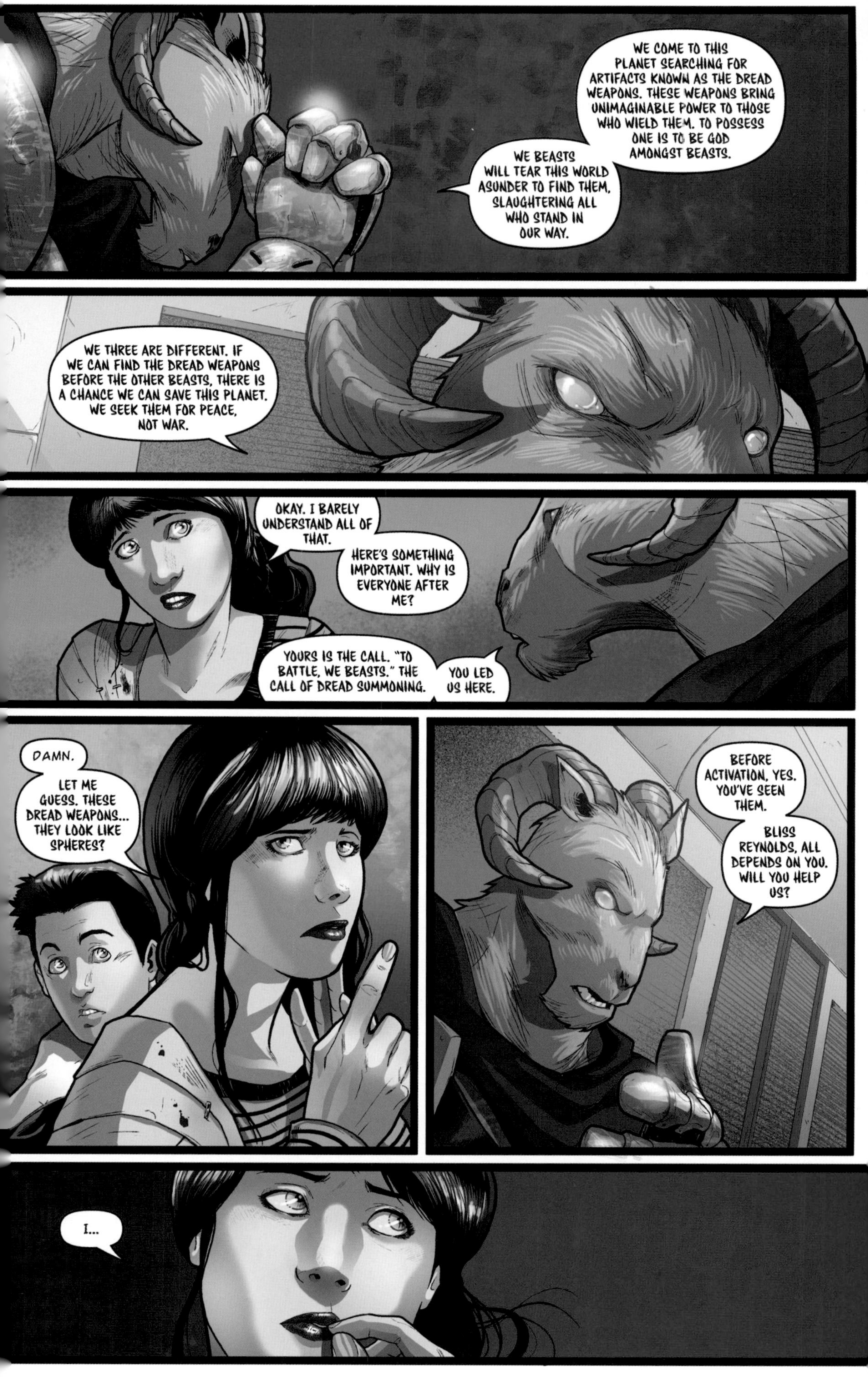

WE COME TO THIS PLANET SEARCHING FOR ARTIFACTS KNOWN AS THE DREAD WEAPONS. THESE WEAPONS BRING UNIMAGINABLE POWER TO THOSE WHO WIELD THEM. TO POSSESS ONE IS TO BE GOD AMONGST BEASTS.
WE BEASTS WILL TEAR THIS WORLD ASUNDER TO FIND THEM, SLAUGHTERING ALL WHO STAND IN OUR WAY.
WE THREE ARE DIFFERENT. IF WE CAN FIND THE DREAD WEAPONS BEFORE THE OTHER BEASTS, THERE IS A CHANCE WE CAN SAVE THIS PLANET. WE SEEK THEM FOR PEACE, NOT WAR.
OKAY. I BARELY UNDERSTAND ALL OF THAT.
HERE'S SOMETHING IMPORTANT. WHY IS EVERYONE AFTER ME?
YOURS IS THE CALL. "TO BATTLE, WE BEASTS." THE CALL OF DREAD SUMMONING.
YOU LED US HERE.
DAMN.
LET ME GUESS. THESE DREAD WEAPONS... THEY LOOK LIKE SPHERES?
BEFORE ACTIVATION, YES. YOU'VE SEEN THEM.
BLISS REYNOLDS, ALL DEPENDS ON YOU. WILL YOU HELP US?
I...

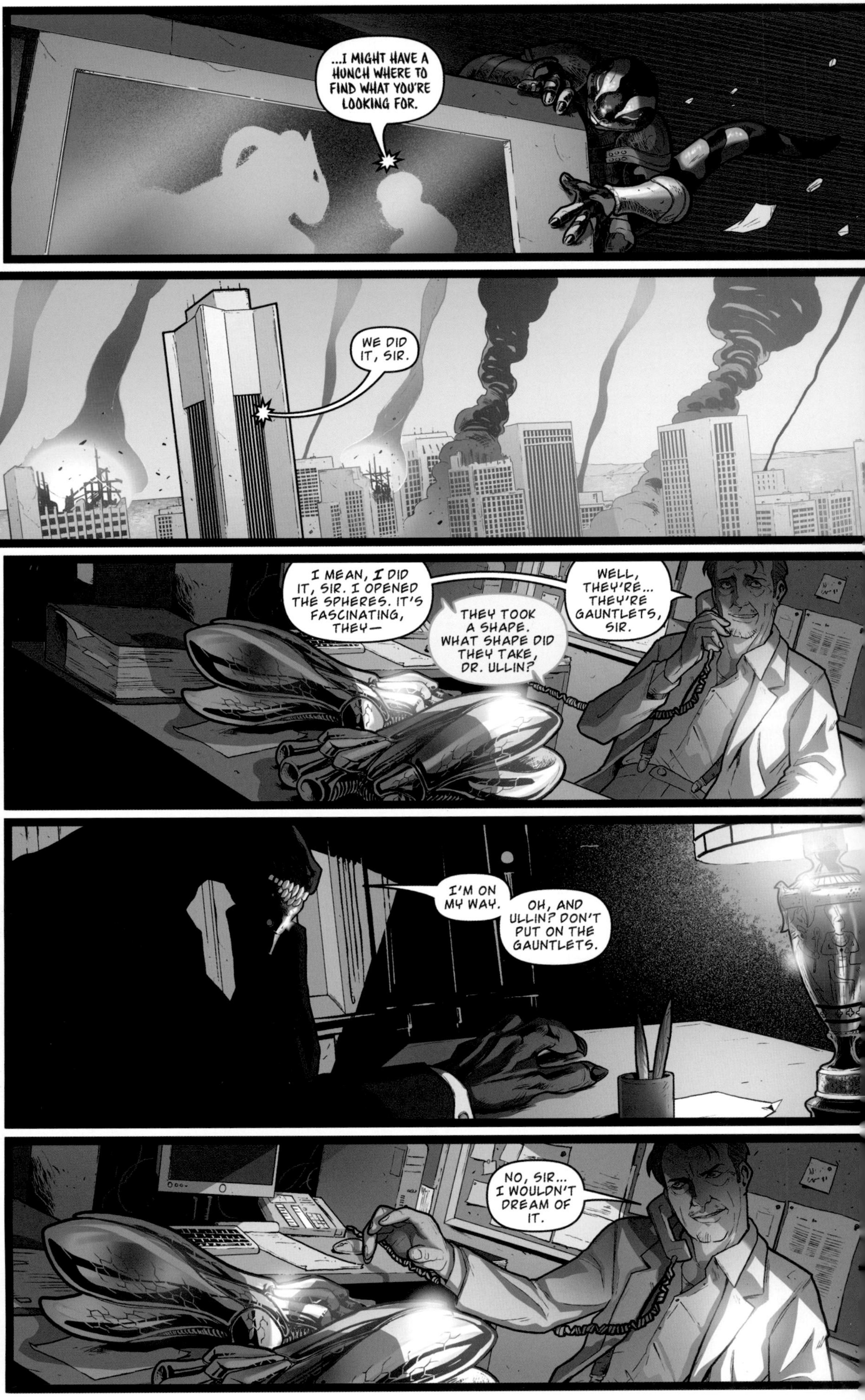
...I MIGHT HAVE A HUNCH WHERE TO FIND WHAT YOU'RE LOOKING FOR.
WE DID IT, SIR.
I MEAN, I DID IT, SIR. I OPENED THE SPHERES. IT'S FASCINATING, THEY—
THEY TOOK A SHAPE. WHAT SHAPE DID THEY TAKE, DR. ULLIN?
WELL, THEY'RE... THEY'RE GAUNTLETS, SIR.
I'M ON MY WAY.
OH, AND ULLIN? DON'T PUT ON THE GAUNTLETS.
NO, SIR... I WOULDN'T DREAM OF IT.

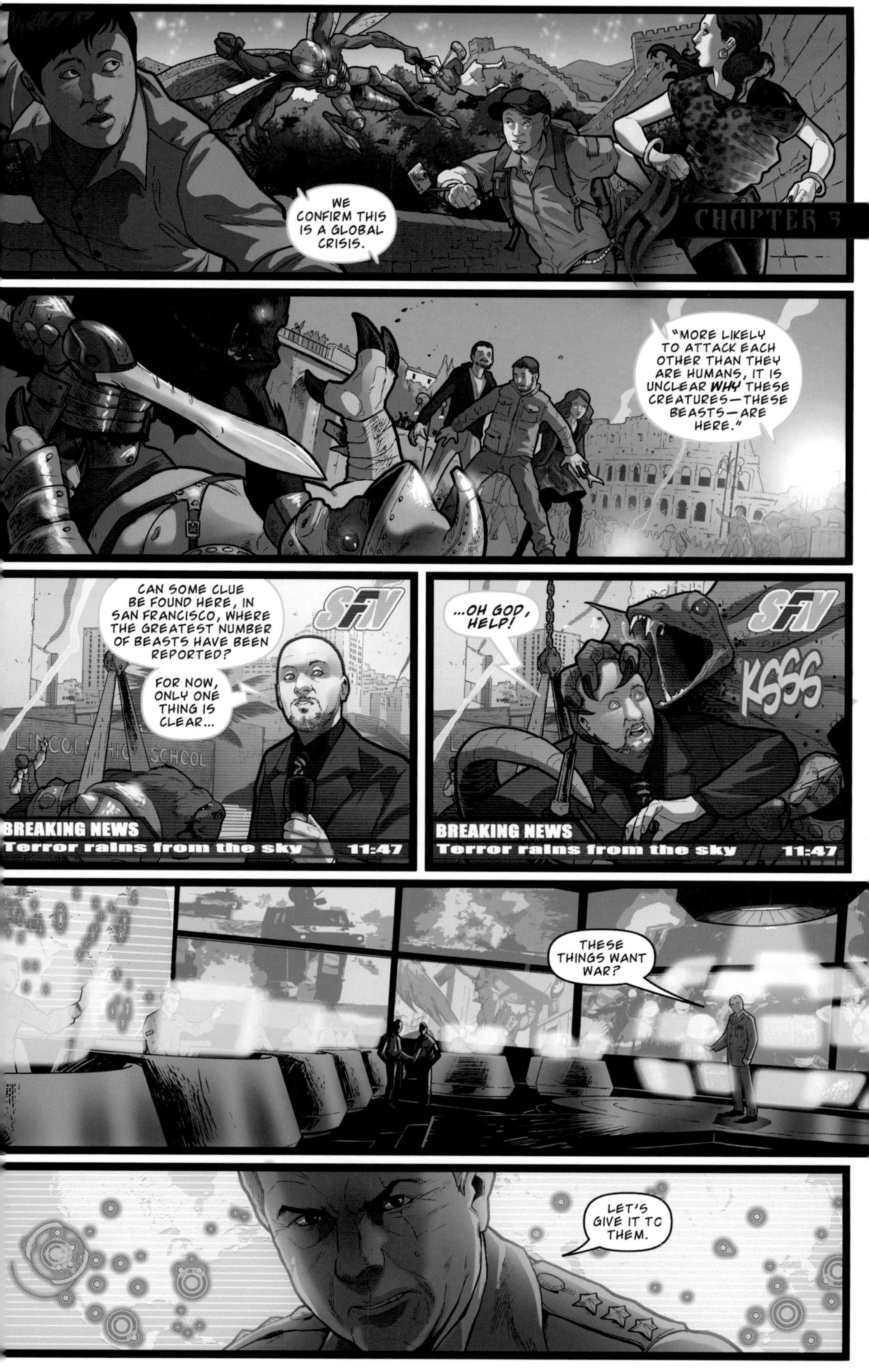
WE CONFIRM THIS IS A GLOBAL CRISIS.
CHAPTER 3
"MORE LIKELY TO ATTACK EACH OTHER THAN THEY ARE HUMANS, IT IS UNCLEAR WHY THESE CREATURES—THESE BEASTS—ARE HERE."
CAN SOME CLUE BE FOUND HERE, IN SAN FRANCISCO, WHERE THE GREATEST NUMBER OF BEASTS HAVE BEEN REPORTED?
FOR NOW, ONLY ONE THING IS CLEAR...
SFN
BREAKING NEWS
Terror rains from the sky
11:47
...OH GOD, HELP!
SFN
KSSS
BREAKING NEWS
Terror rains from the sky
11:47
THESE THINGS WANT WAR?
LET'S GIVE IT TO THEM.

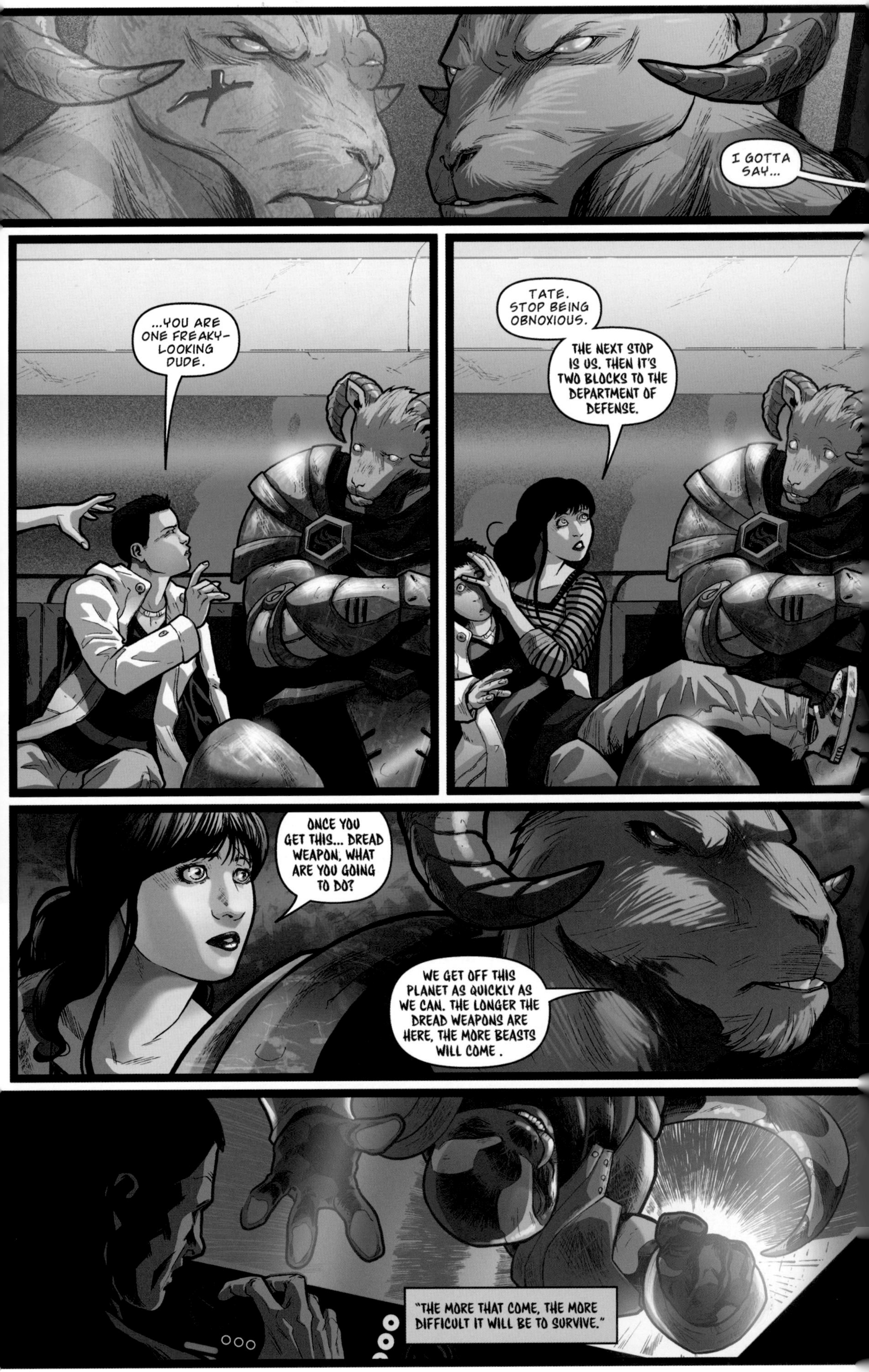
I GOTTA SAY...
...YOU ARE ONE FREAKY-LOOKING DUDE.
TATE. STOP BEING OBNOXIOUS.
THE NEXT STOP IS US. THEN IT'S TWO BLOCKS TO THE DEPARTMENT OF DEFENSE.
ONCE YOU GET THIS... DREAD WEAPON, WHAT ARE YOU GOING TO DO?
WE GET OFF THIS PLANET AS QUICKLY AS WE CAN. THE LONGER THE DREAD WEAPONS ARE HERE, THE MORE BEASTS WILL COME.
"THE MORE THAT COME, THE MORE DIFFICULT IT WILL BE TO SURVIVE."

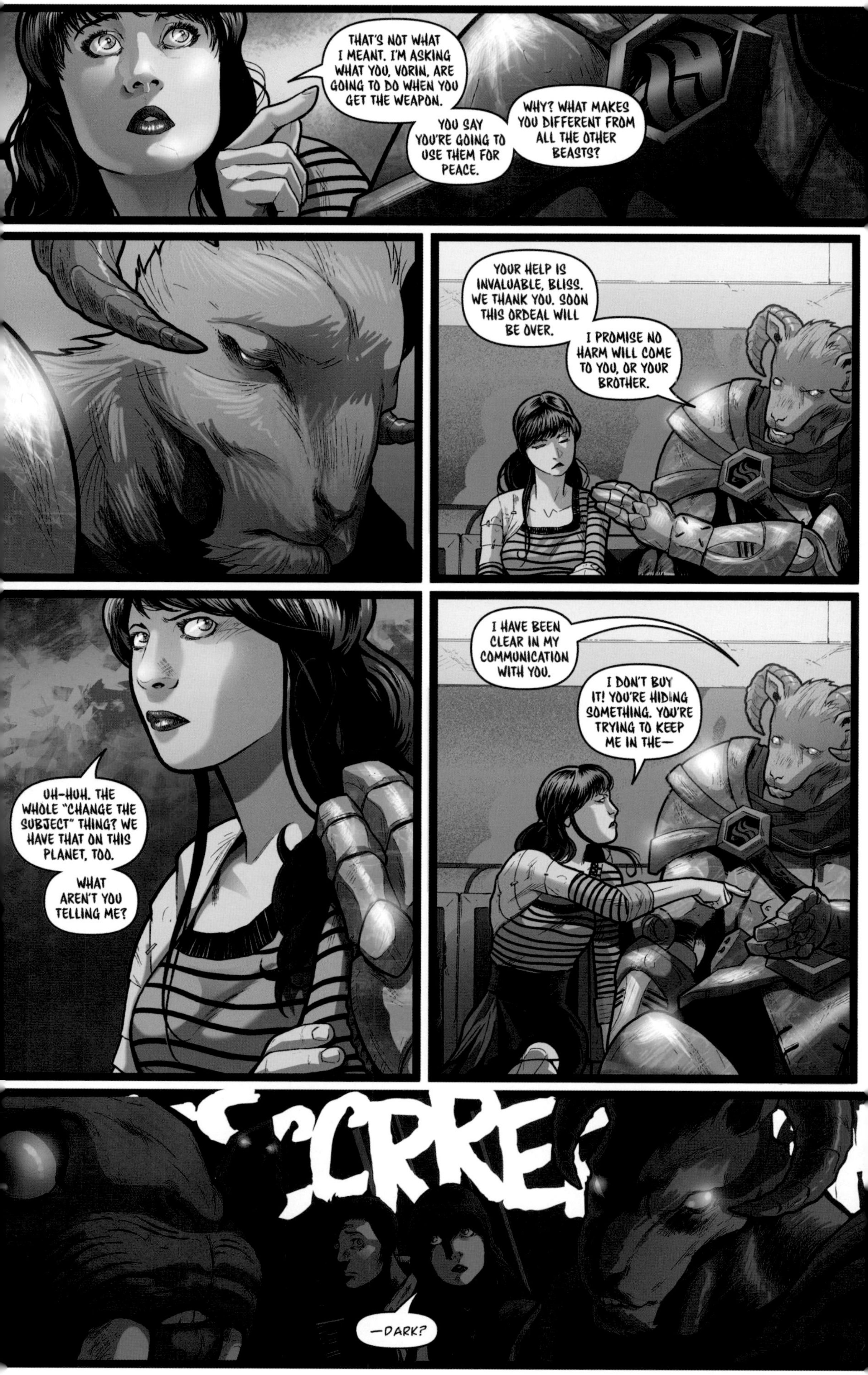
THAT'S NOT WHAT I MEANT. I'M ASKING WHAT YOU, VORIN, ARE GOING TO DO WHEN YOU GET THE WEAPON.
YOU SAY YOU'RE GOING TO USE THEM FOR PEACE.
WHY? WHAT MAKES YOU DIFFERENT FROM ALL THE OTHER BEASTS?
YOUR HELP IS INVALUABLE, BLISS. WE THANK YOU. SOON THIS ORDEAL WILL BE OVER.
I PROMISE NO HARM WILL COME TO YOU, OR YOUR BROTHER.
UH-HUH. THE WHOLE "CHANGE THE SUBJECT" THING? WE HAVE THAT ON THIS PLANET, TOO.
WHAT AREN'T YOU TELLING ME?
I HAVE BEEN CLEAR IN MY COMMUNICATION WITH YOU.
I DON'T BUY IT! YOU'RE HIDING SOMETHING. YOU'RE TRYING TO KEEP ME IN THE—
—DARK?

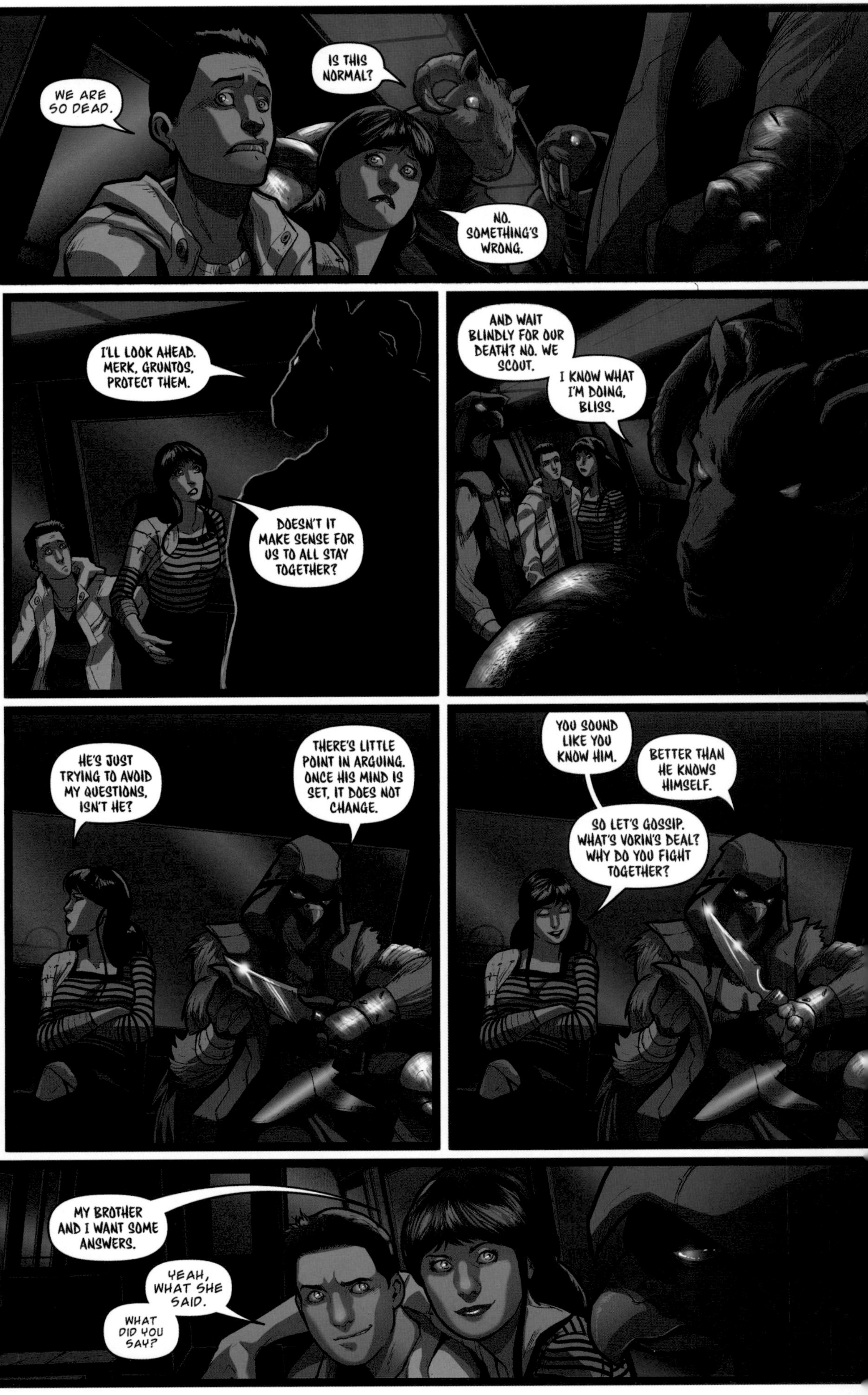
WE ARE SO DEAD.
IS THIS NORMAL?
NO. SOMETHING'S WRONG.
I'LL LOOK AHEAD. MERK, GRUNTOS, PROTECT THEM.
DOESN'T IT MAKE SENSE FOR US TO ALL STAY TOGETHER?
AND WAIT BLINDLY FOR OUR DEATH? NO. WE SCOUT.
I KNOW WHAT I'M DOING, BLISS.
HE'S JUST TRYING TO AVOID MY QUESTIONS, ISN'T HE?
THERE'S LITTLE POINT IN ARGUING. ONCE HIS MIND IS SET, IT DOES NOT CHANGE.
YOU SOUND LIKE YOU KNOW HIM.
BETTER THAN HE KNOWS HIMSELF.
SO LET'S GOSSIP. WHAT'S VORIN'S DEAL? WHY DO YOU FIGHT TOGETHER?
MY BROTHER AND I WANT SOME ANSWERS.
YEAH, WHAT SHE SAID.
WHAT DID YOU SAY?

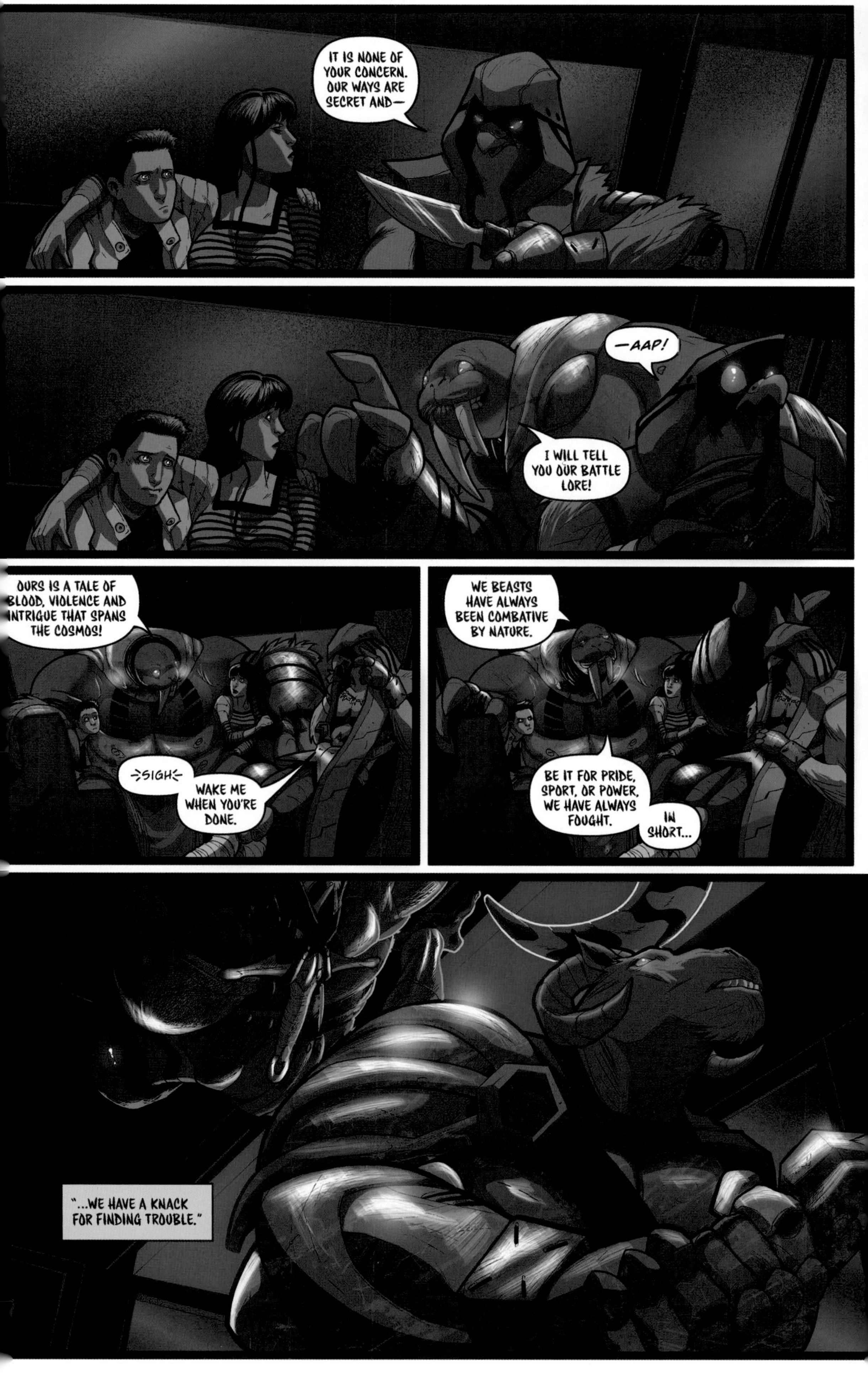
IT IS NONE OF YOUR CONCERN. OUR WAYS ARE SECRET AND—
—AAP!
I WILL TELL YOU OUR BATTLE LORE!
OURS IS A TALE OF BLOOD, VIOLENCE AND INTRIGUE THAT SPANS THE COSMOS!
SIGH
WAKE ME WHEN YOU'RE DONE.
WE BEASTS HAVE ALWAYS BEEN COMBATIVE BY NATURE.
BE IT FOR PRIDE, SPORT, OR POWER, WE HAVE ALWAYS FOUGHT.
IN SHORT...
"...WE HAVE A KNACK FOR FINDING TROUBLE."

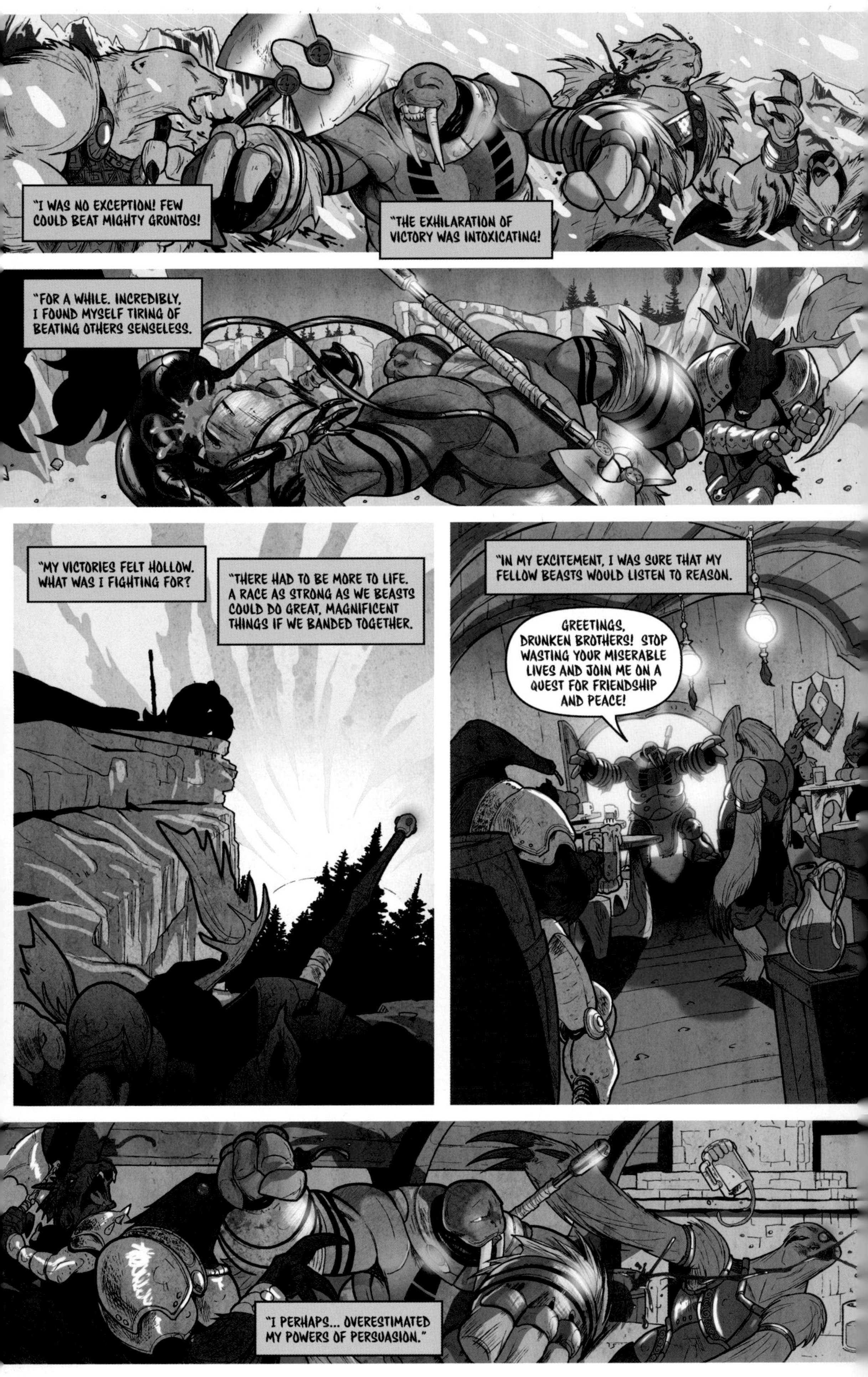
"I WAS NO EXCEPTION! FEW COULD BEAT MIGHTY GRUNTOS!
"THE EXHILARATION OF VICTORY WAS INTOXICATING!
"FOR A WHILE. INCREDIBLY, I FOUND MYSELF TIRING OF BEATING OTHERS SENSELESS.
"MY VICTORIES FELT HOLLOW. WHAT WAS I FIGHTING FOR?
"THERE HAD TO BE MORE TO LIFE. A RACE AS STRONG AS WE BEASTS COULD DO GREAT, MAGNIFICENT THINGS IF WE BANDED TOGETHER.
"IN MY EXCITEMENT, I WAS SURE THAT MY FELLOW BEASTS WOULD LISTEN TO REASON.
GREETINGS, DRUNKEN BROTHERS! STOP WASTING YOUR MISERABLE LIVES AND JOIN ME ON A QUEST FOR FRIENDSHIP AND PEACE!
"I PERHAPS... OVERESTIMATED MY POWERS OF PERSUASION."

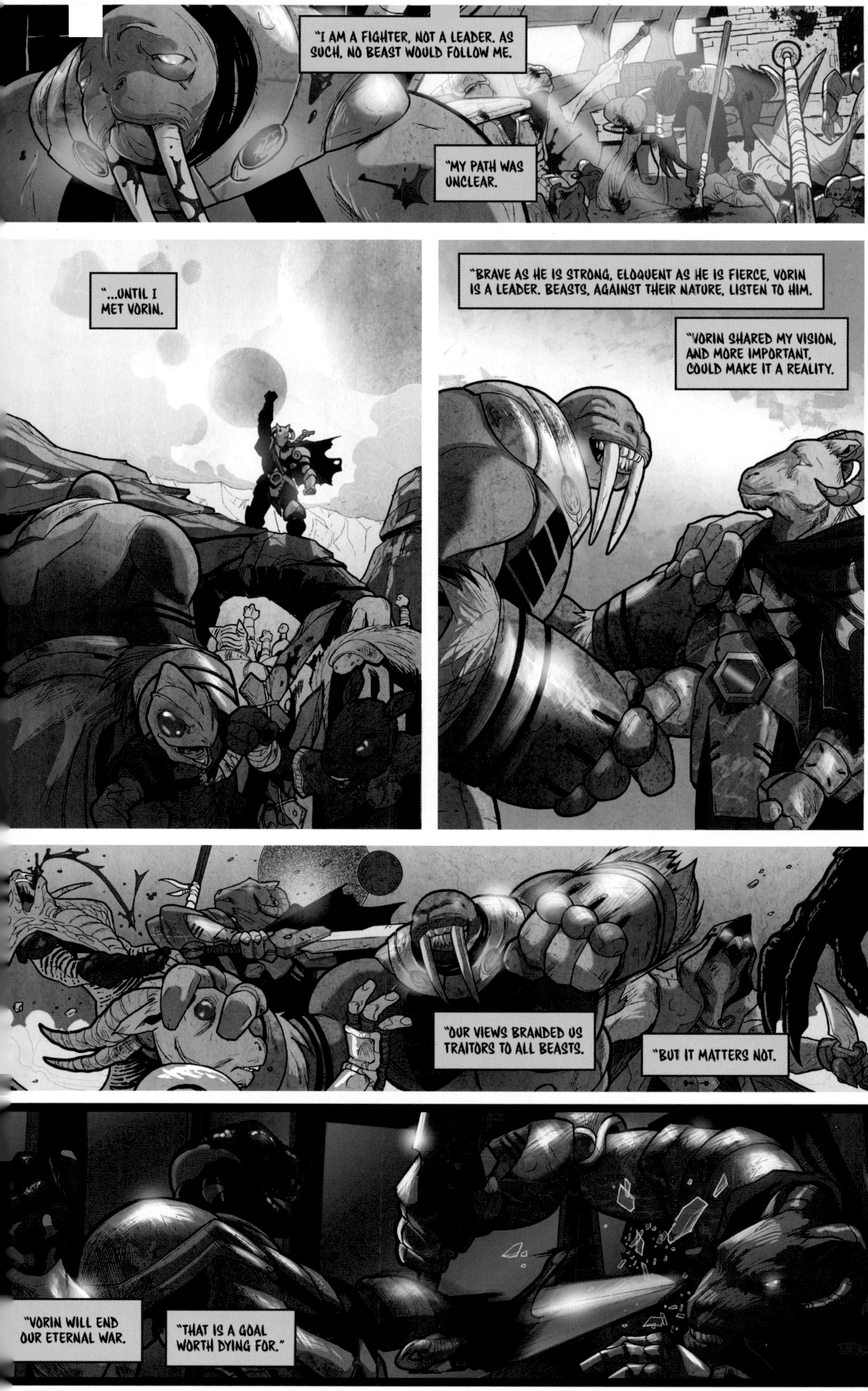
"I AM A FIGHTER, NOT A LEADER. AS SUCH, NO BEAST WOULD FOLLOW ME.
"MY PATH WAS UNCLEAR.
"...UNTIL I MET VORIN.
"BRAVE AS HE IS STRONG, ELOQUENT AS HE IS FIERCE, VORIN IS A LEADER. BEASTS, AGAINST THEIR NATURE, LISTEN TO HIM.
"VORIN SHARED MY VISION, AND MORE IMPORTANT, COULD MAKE IT A REALITY.
"OUR VIEWS BRANDED US TRAITORS TO ALL BEASTS.
"BUT IT MATTERS NOT.
"VORIN WILL END OUR ETERNAL WAR.
"THAT IS A GOAL WORTH DYING FOR."

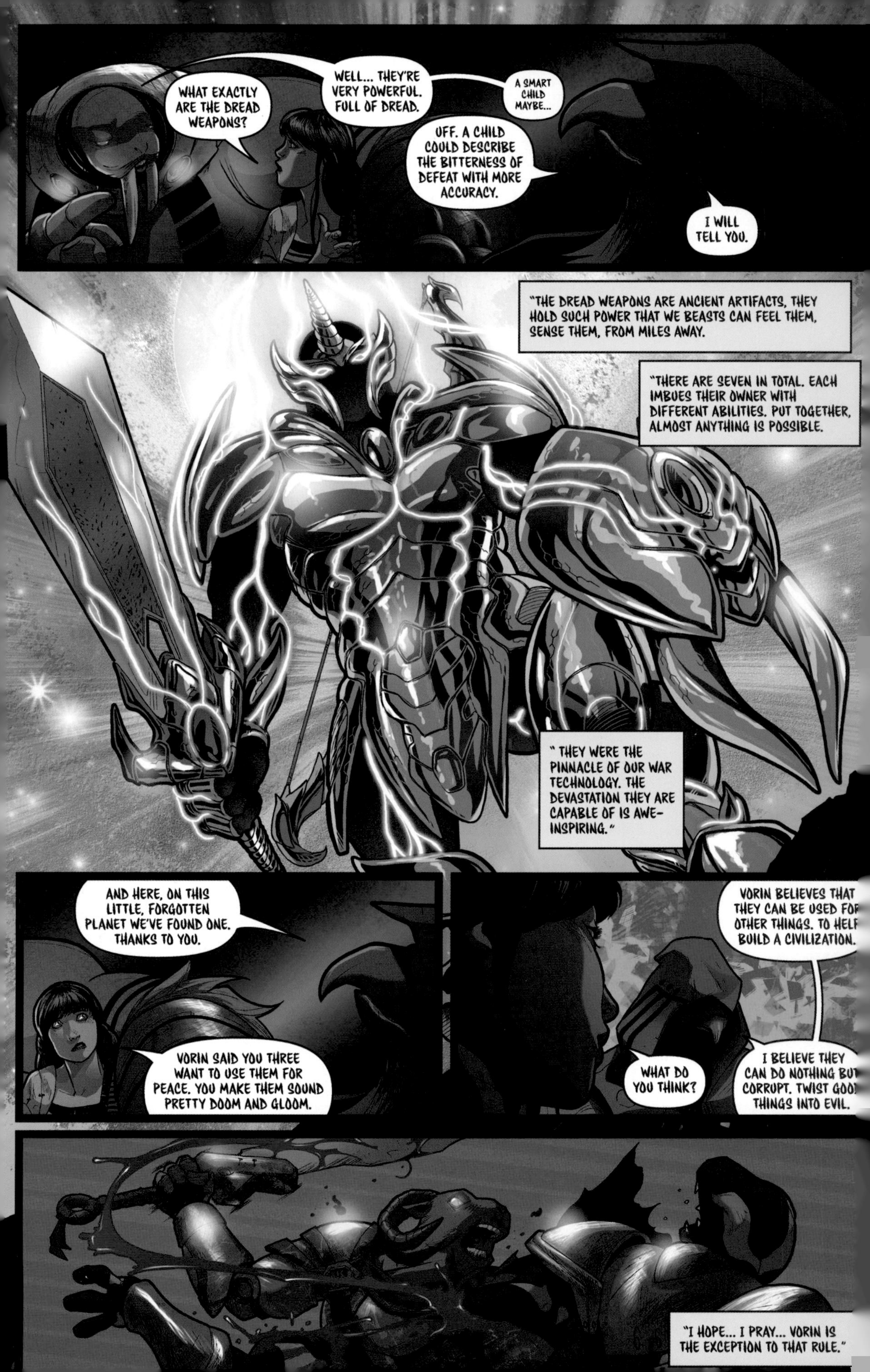
WHAT EXACTLY ARE THE DREAD WEAPONS?
WELL... THEY'RE VERY POWERFUL. FULL OF DREAD.
A SMART CHILD MAYBE...
UFF. A CHILD COULD DESCRIBE THE BITTERNESS OF DEFEAT WITH MORE ACCURACY.
I WILL TELL YOU.
"THE DREAD WEAPONS ARE ANCIENT ARTIFACTS, THEY HOLD SUCH POWER THAT WE BEASTS CAN FEEL THEM, SENSE THEM, FROM MILES AWAY.
"THERE ARE SEVEN IN TOTAL. EACH IMBUES THEIR OWNER WITH DIFFERENT ABILITIES. PUT TOGETHER, ALMOST ANYTHING IS POSSIBLE.
" THEY WERE THE PINNACLE OF OUR WAR TECHNOLOGY. THE DEVASTATION THEY ARE CAPABLE OF IS AWE-INSPIRING."
AND HERE, ON THIS LITTLE, FORGOTTEN PLANET WE'VE FOUND ONE. THANKS TO YOU.
VORIN SAID YOU THREE WANT TO USE THEM FOR PEACE. YOU MAKE THEM SOUND PRETTY DOOM AND GLOOM.
VORIN BELIEVES THAT THEY CAN BE USED FOR OTHER THINGS. TO HELP BUILD A CIVILIZATION.
WHAT DO YOU THINK?
I BELIEVE THEY CAN DO NOTHING BUT CORRUPT. TWIST GOOD THINGS INTO EVIL.
"I HOPE... I PRAY... VORIN IS THE EXCEPTION TO THAT RULE."

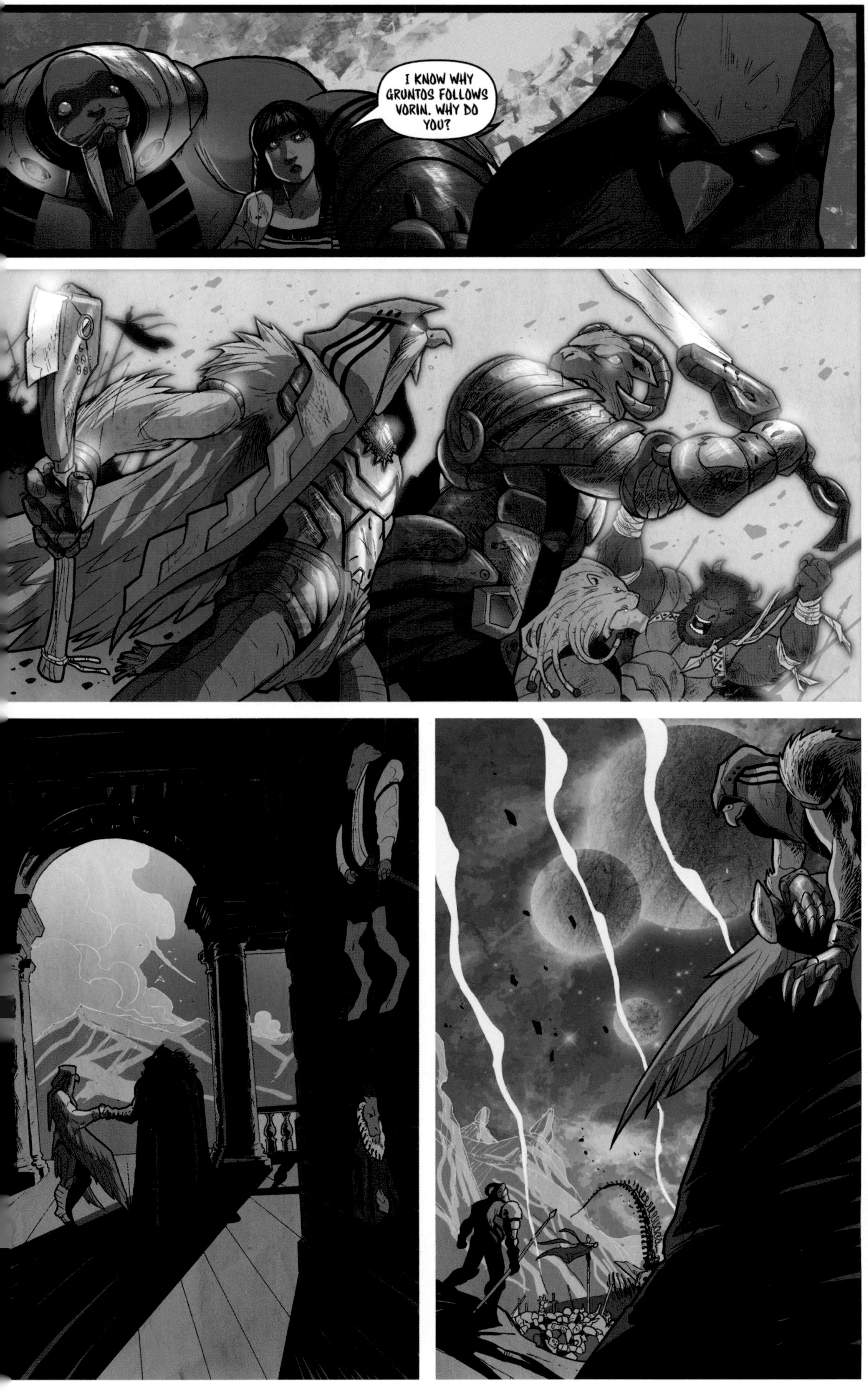
I KNOW WHY GRUNTOS FOLLOWS VORIN. WHY DO YOU?

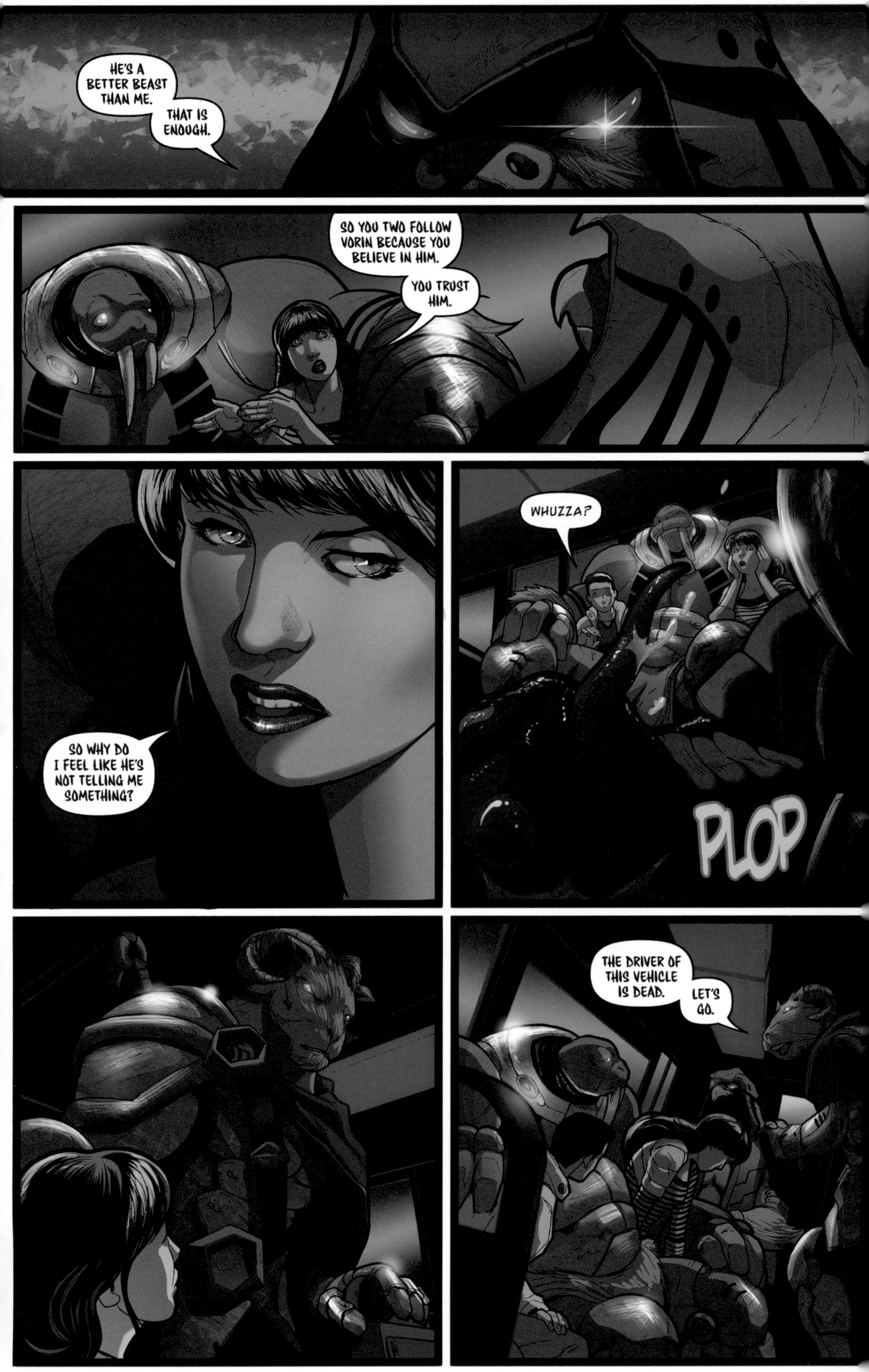
HE'S A BETTER BEAST THAN ME.
THAT IS ENOUGH.
SO YOU TWO FOLLOW VORIN BECAUSE YOU BELIEVE IN HIM.
YOU TRUST HIM.
SO WHY DO I FEEL LIKE HE'S NOT TELLING ME SOMETHING?
WHUZZA?
PLOP!
THE DRIVER OF THIS VEHICLE IS DEAD.
LET'S GO.

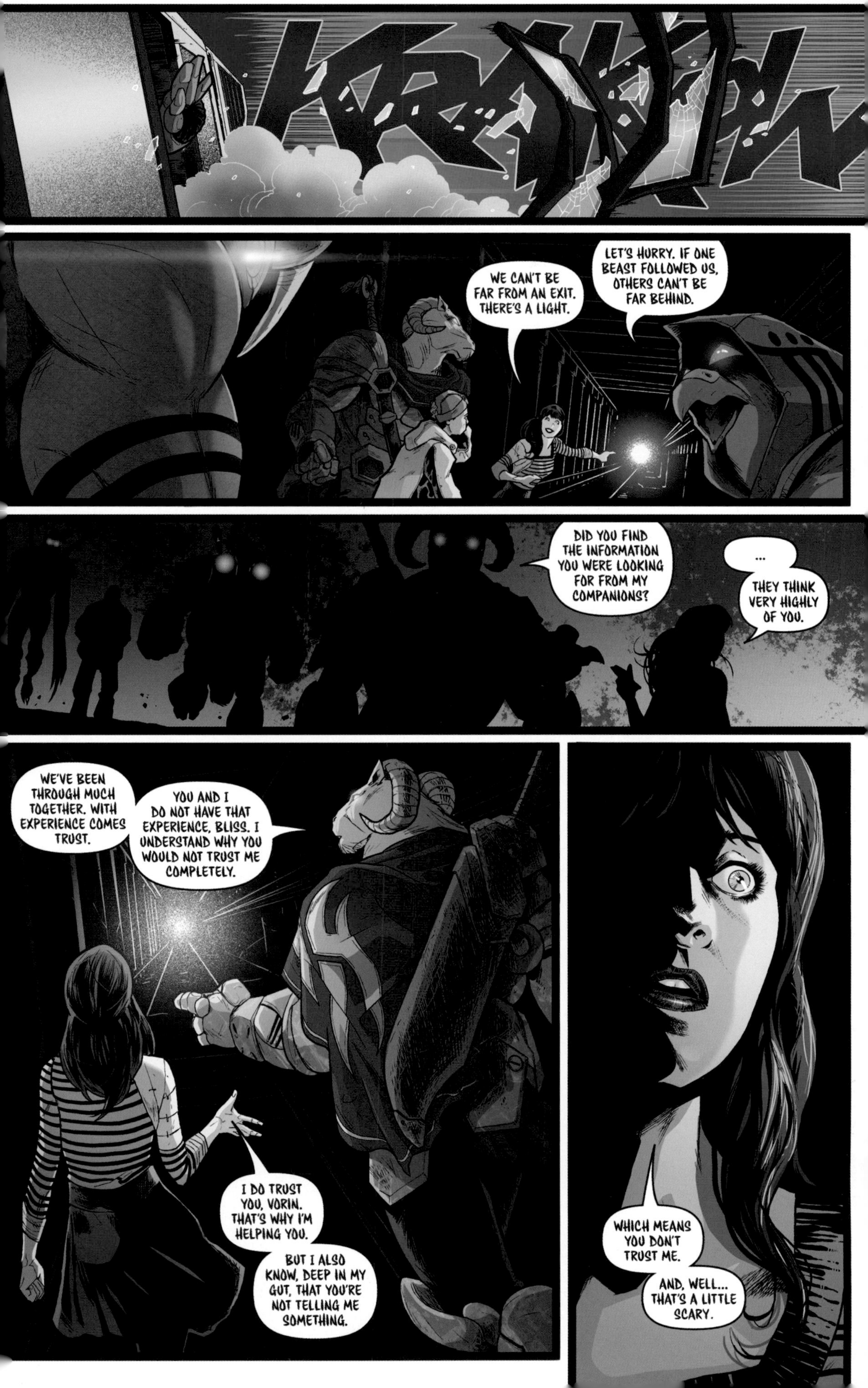
WE CAN'T BE FAR FROM AN EXIT. THERE'S A LIGHT.
LET'S HURRY. IF ONE BEAST FOLLOWED US, OTHERS CAN'T BE FAR BEHIND.
DID YOU FIND THE INFORMATION YOU WERE LOOKING FOR FROM MY COMPANIONS?
...
THEY THINK VERY HIGHLY OF YOU.
WE'VE BEEN THROUGH MUCH TOGETHER. WITH EXPERIENCE COMES TRUST.
YOU AND I DO NOT HAVE THAT EXPERIENCE, BLISS. I UNDERSTAND WHY YOU WOULD NOT TRUST ME COMPLETELY.
I DO TRUST YOU, VORIN. THAT'S WHY I'M HELPING YOU.
BUT I ALSO KNOW, DEEP IN MY GUT, THAT YOU'RE NOT TELLING ME SOMETHING.
WHICH MEANS YOU DON'T TRUST ME.
AND, WELL... THAT'S A LITTLE SCARY.

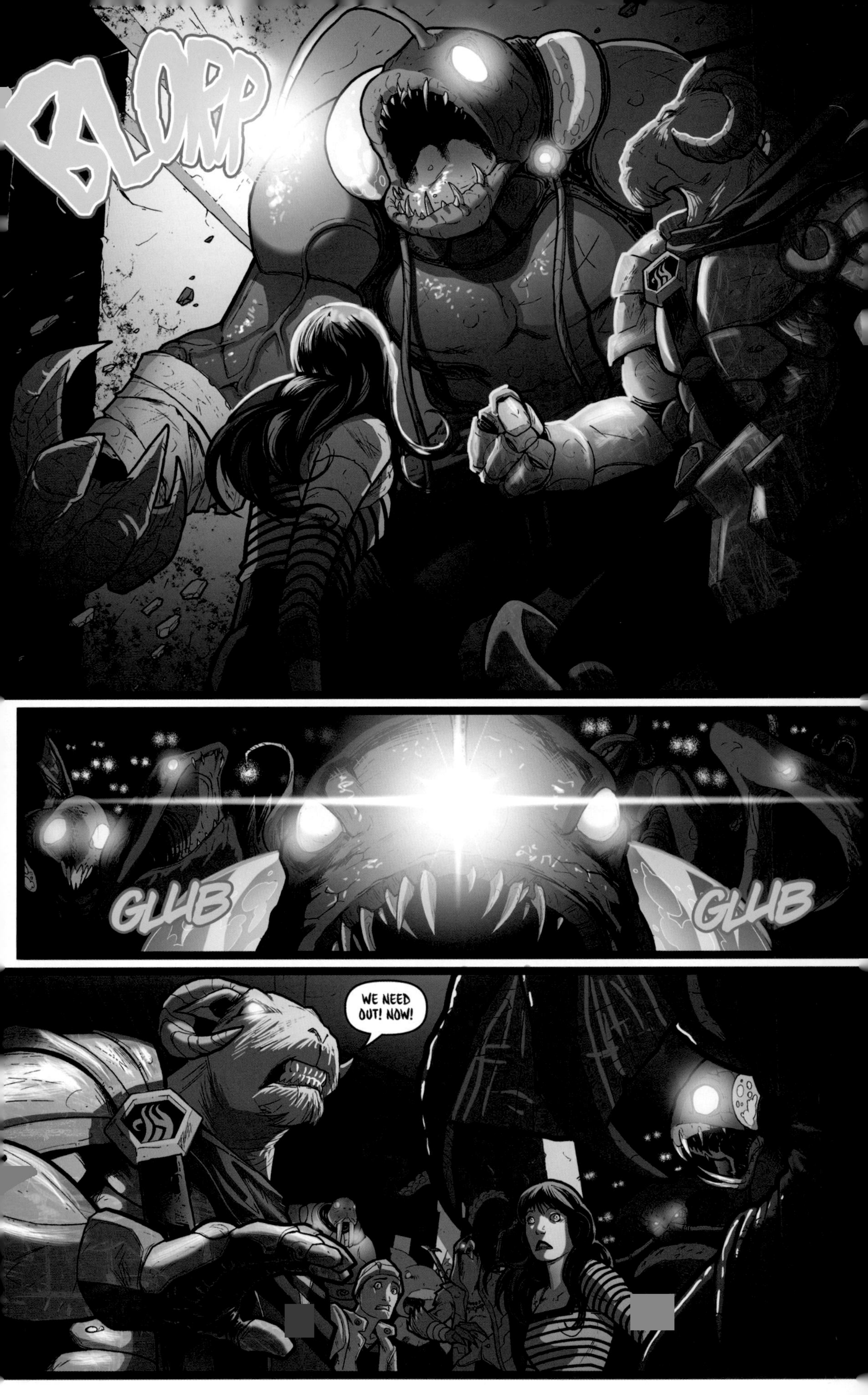
BLORP
GLUB
GLUB
WE NEED OUT! NOW!

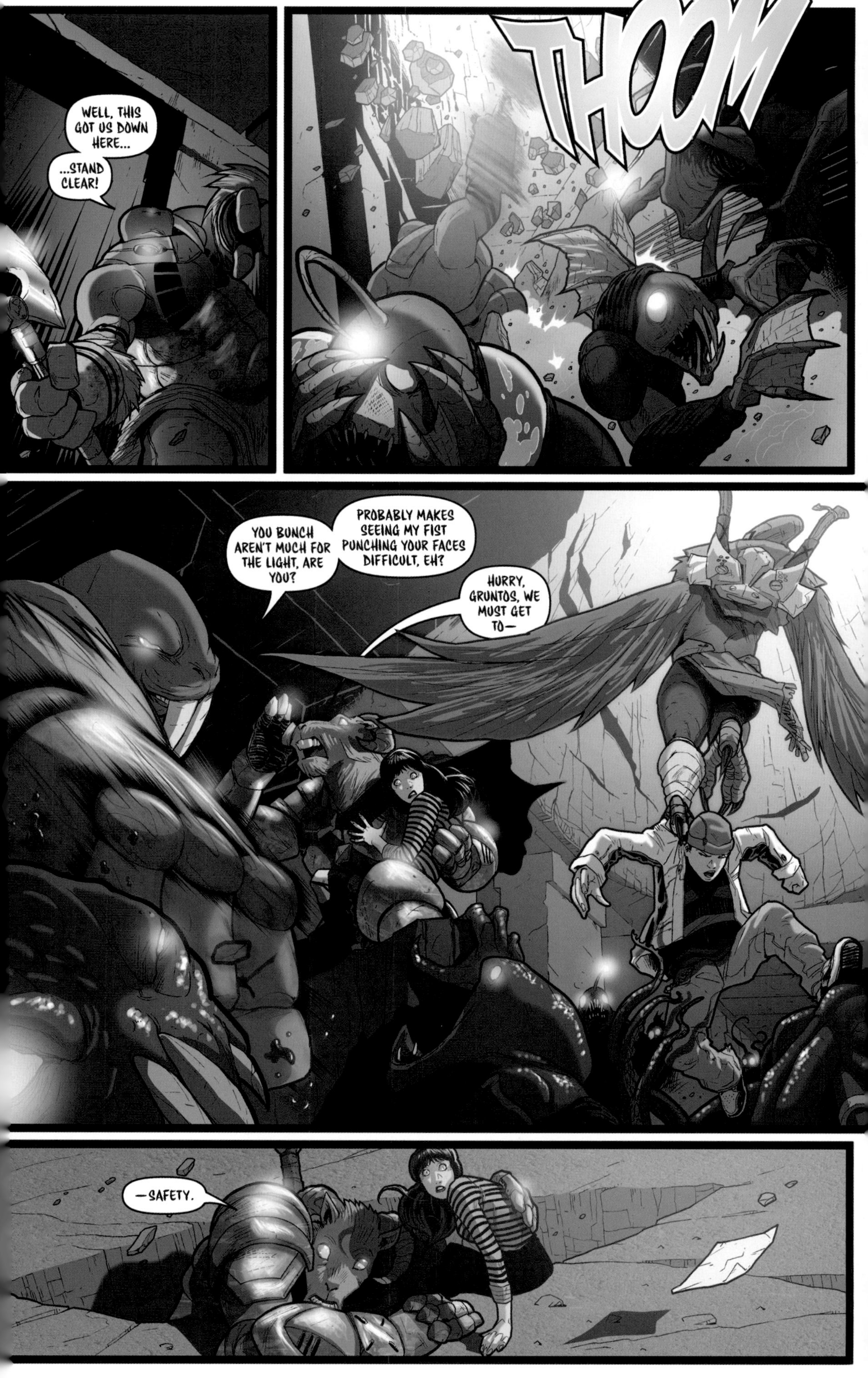
WELL, THIS GOT US DOWN HERE...
...STAND CLEAR!
THOOM
YOU BUNCH AREN'T MUCH FOR THE LIGHT, ARE YOU?
PROBABLY MAKES SEEING MY FIST PUNCHING YOUR FACES DIFFICULT, EH?
HURRY, GRUNTOS, WE MUST GET TO—
—SAFETY.

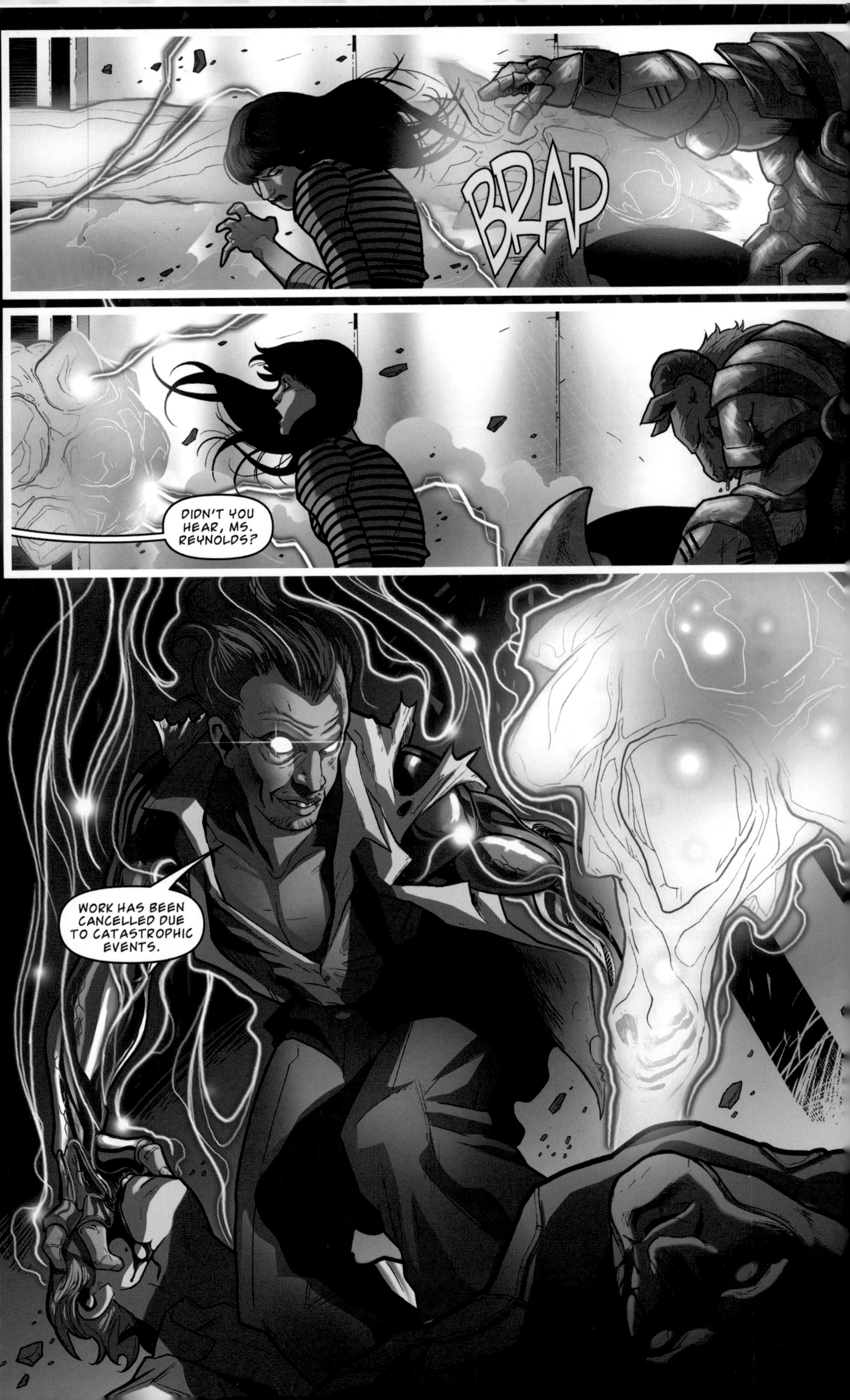
BRAP
DIDN'T YOU HEAR, MS. REYNOLDS?
WORK HAS BEEN CANCELLED DUE TO CATASTROPHIC EVENTS.

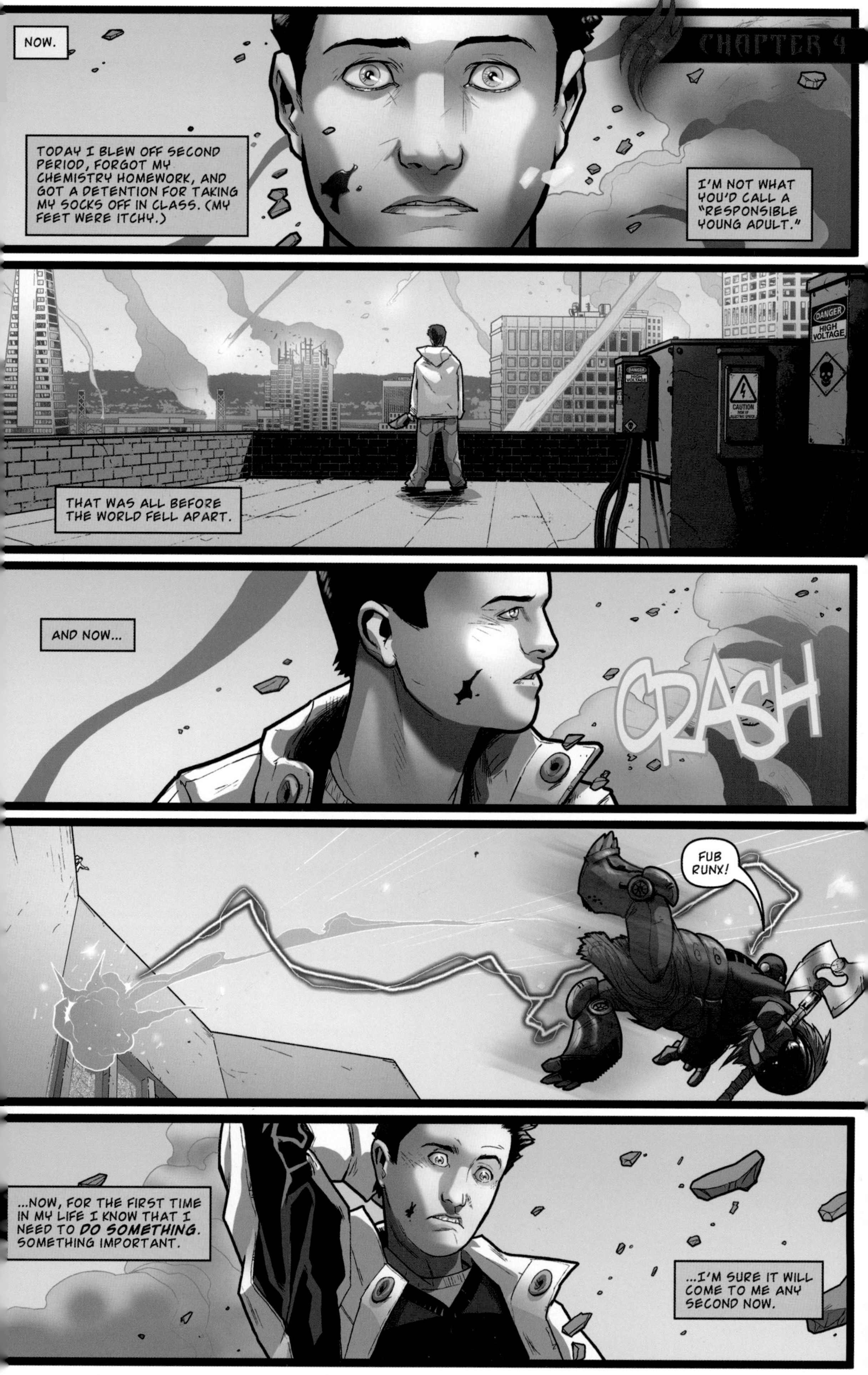
CHAPTER 4
NOW.
TODAY I BLEW OFF SECOND PERIOD, FORGOT MY CHEMISTRY HOMEWORK, AND GOT A DETENTION FOR TAKING MY SOCKS OFF IN CLASS. (MY FEET WERE ITCHY.)
I'M NOT WHAT YOU'D CALL A "RESPONSIBLE YOUNG ADULT."
DANGER HIGH VOLTAGE
CAUTION
THAT WAS ALL BEFORE THE WORLD FELL APART.
AND NOW...
CRASH
FUB RUNX!
...NOW, FOR THE FIRST TIME IN MY LIFE I KNOW THAT I NEED TO DO SOMETHING. SOMETHING IMPORTANT.
...I'M SURE IT WILL COME TO ME ANY SECOND NOW.

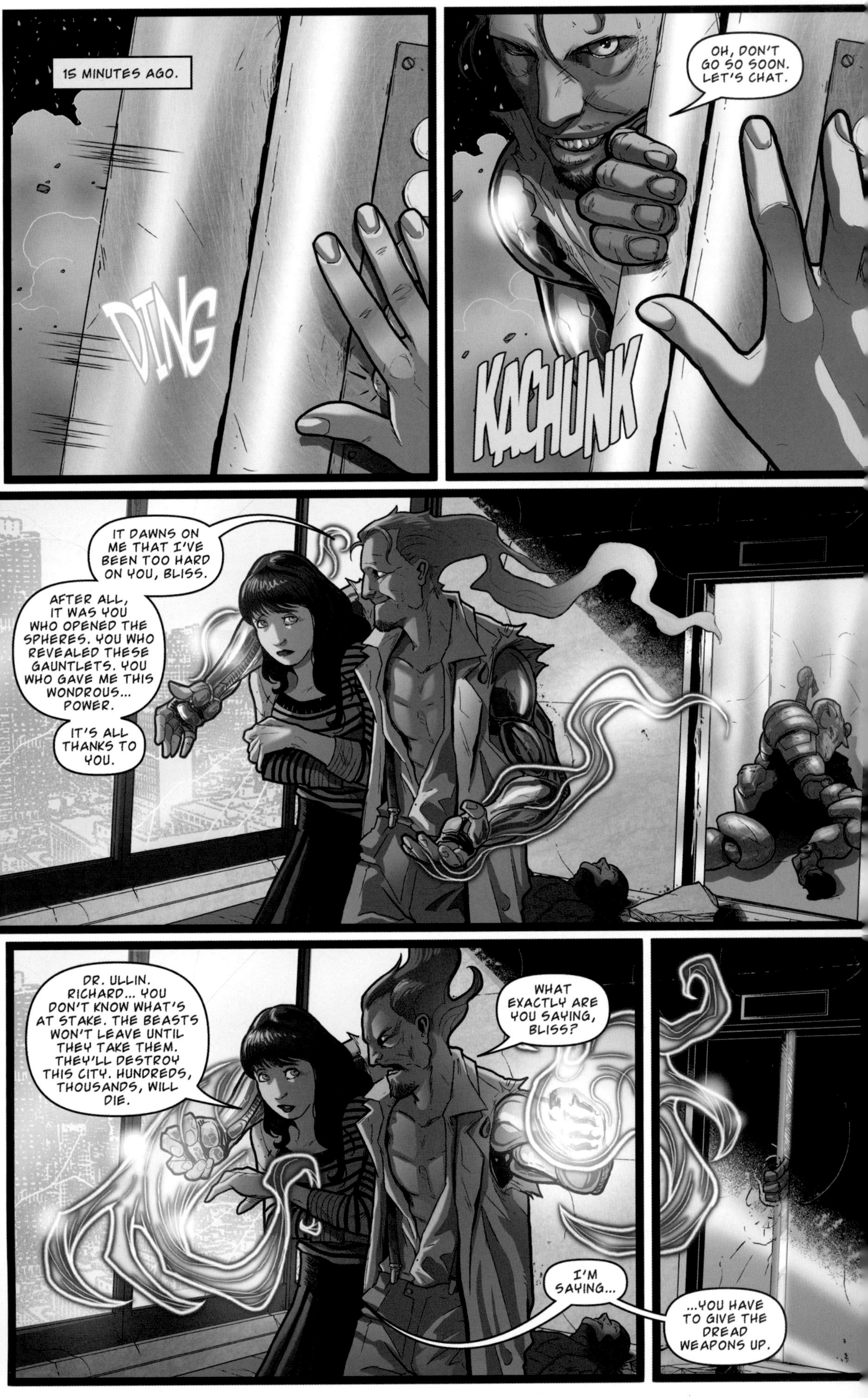
15 MINUTES AGO.
DING
OH, DON'T GO SO SOON. LET'S CHAT.
KACHUNK
IT DAWNS ON ME THAT I'VE BEEN TOO HARD ON YOU, BLISS.
AFTER ALL, IT WAS YOU WHO OPENED THE SPHERES. YOU WHO REVEALED THESE GAUNTLETS. YOU WHO GAVE ME THIS WONDROUS... POWER.
IT'S ALL THANKS TO YOU.
DR. ULLIN. RICHARD... YOU DON'T KNOW WHAT'S AT STAKE. THE BEASTS WON'T LEAVE UNTIL THEY TAKE THEM. THEY'LL DESTROY THIS CITY. HUNDREDS, THOUSANDS, WILL DIE.
WHAT EXACTLY ARE YOU SAYING, BLISS?
I'M SAYING...
...YOU HAVE TO GIVE THE DREAD WEAPONS UP.

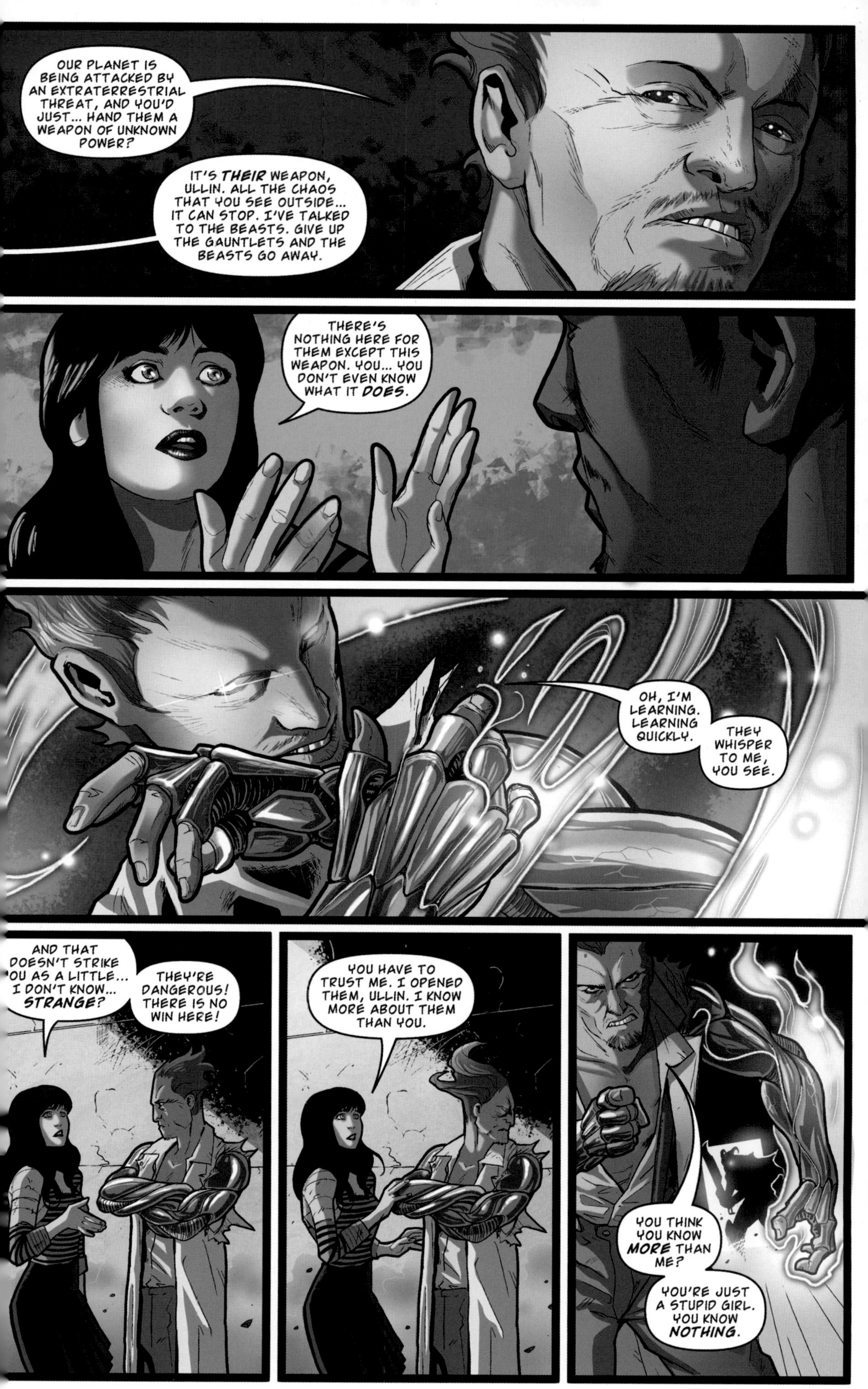
OUR PLANET IS BEING ATTACKED BY AN EXTRATERRESTRIAL THREAT, AND YOU'D JUST... HAND THEM A WEAPON OF UNKNOWN POWER?
IT'S **THEIR** WEAPON, ULLIN. ALL THE CHAOS THAT YOU SEE OUTSIDE... IT CAN STOP. I'VE TALKED TO THE BEASTS. GIVE UP THE GAUNTLETS AND THE BEASTS GO AWAY.
THERE'S NOTHING HERE FOR THEM EXCEPT THIS WEAPON. YOU... YOU DON'T EVEN KNOW WHAT IT **DOES**.
OH, I'M LEARNING. LEARNING QUICKLY.
THEY WHISPER TO ME, YOU SEE.
AND THAT DOESN'T STRIKE OU AS A LITTLE... I DON'T KNOW... **STRANGE**?
THEY'RE DANGEROUS! THERE IS NO WIN HERE!
YOU HAVE TO TRUST ME. I OPENED THEM, ULLIN. I KNOW MORE ABOUT THEM THAN YOU.
YOU THINK YOU KNOW **MORE** THAN ME?
YOU'RE JUST A STUPID GIRL. YOU KNOW **NOTHING**.

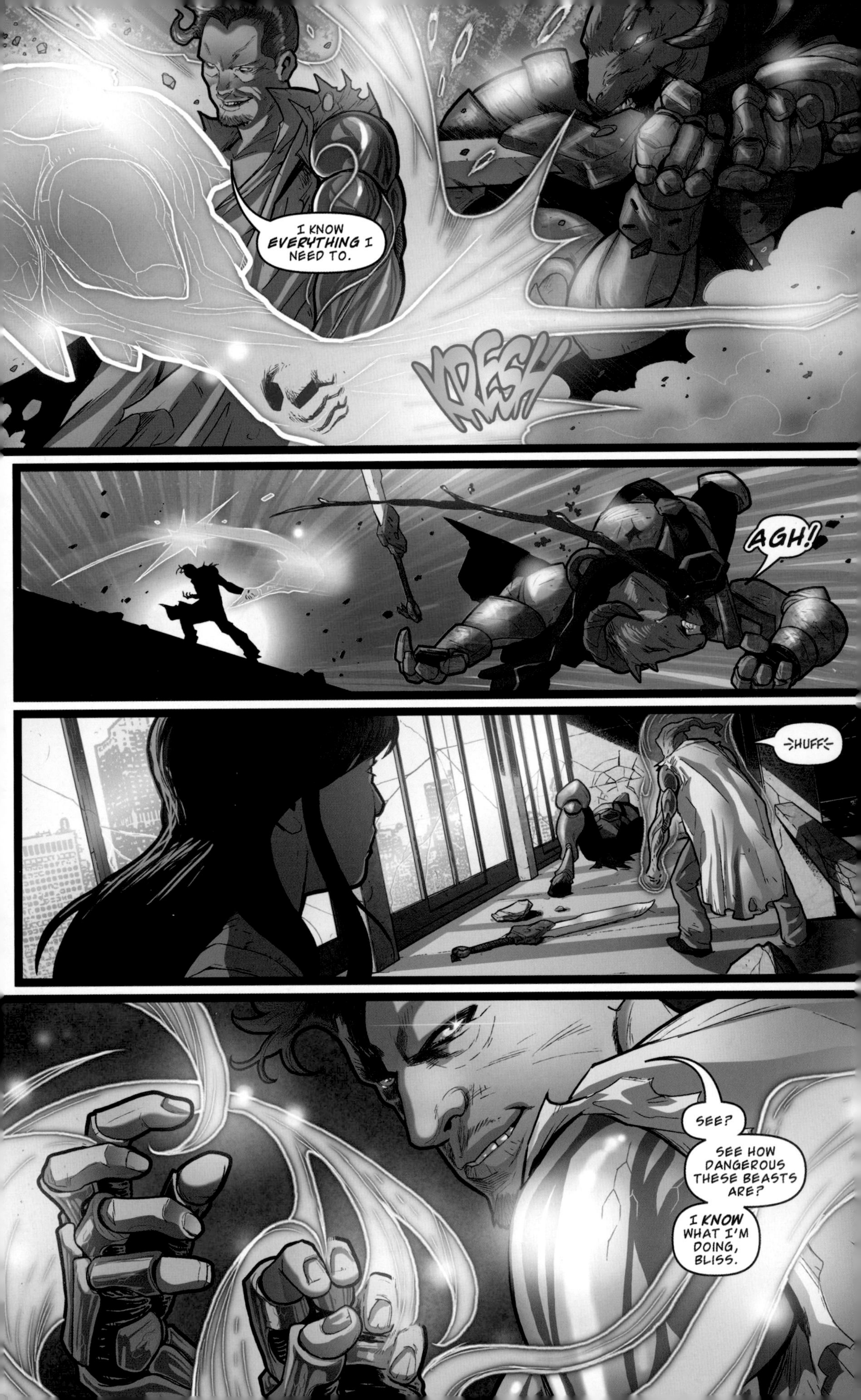
I KNOW EVERYTHING I NEED TO.
KRESH
AGH!
-HUFF-
SEE?
SEE HOW DANGEROUS THESE BEASTS ARE?
I KNOW WHAT I'M DOING, BLISS.

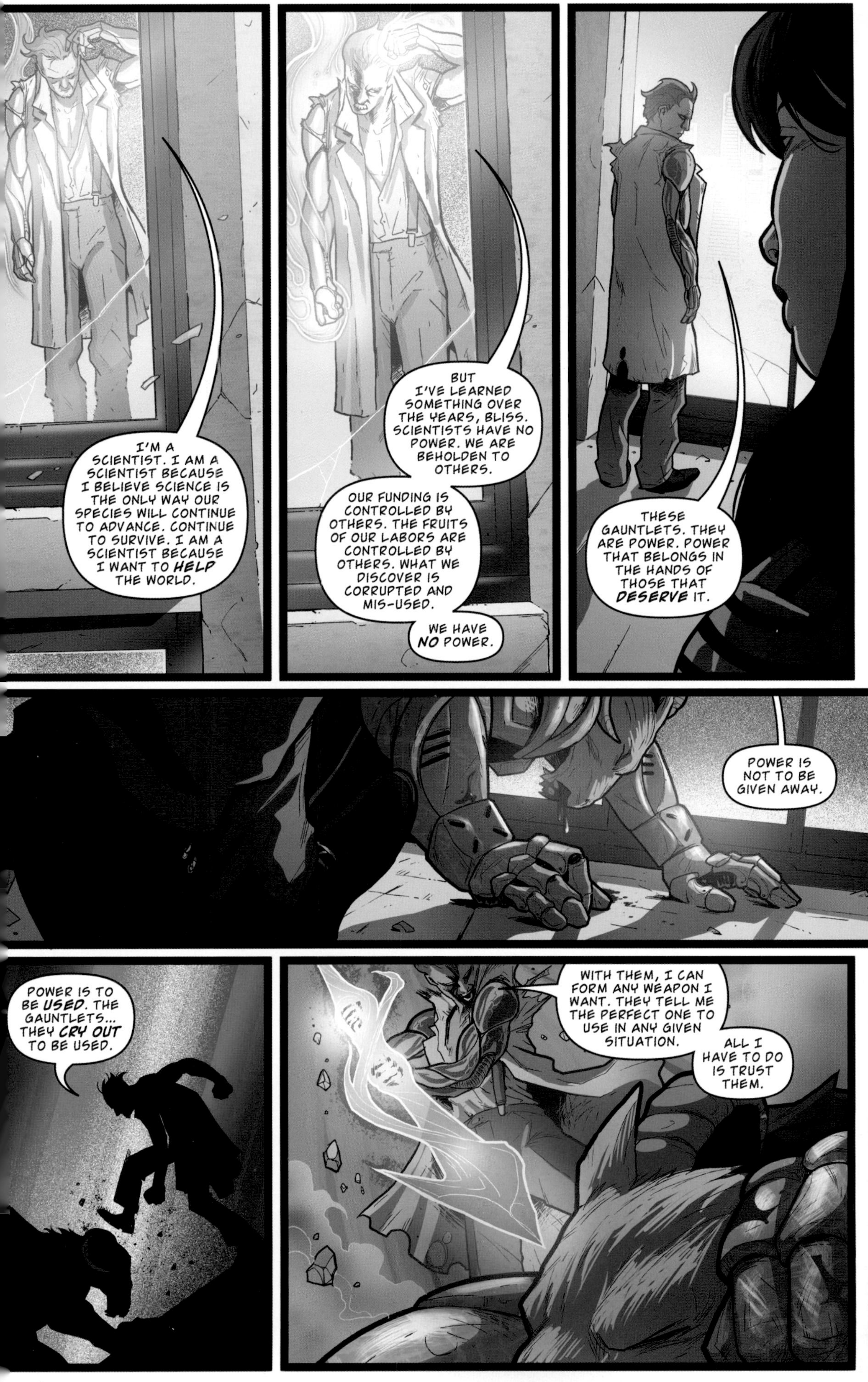
I'M A SCIENTIST. I AM A SCIENTIST BECAUSE I BELIEVE SCIENCE IS THE ONLY WAY OUR SPECIES WILL CONTINUE TO ADVANCE. CONTINUE TO SURVIVE. I AM A SCIENTIST BECAUSE I WANT TO HELP THE WORLD.
BUT I'VE LEARNED SOMETHING OVER THE YEARS, BLISS. SCIENTISTS HAVE NO POWER. WE ARE BEHOLDEN TO OTHERS.
OUR FUNDING IS CONTROLLED BY OTHERS. THE FRUITS OF OUR LABORS ARE CONTROLLED BY OTHERS. WHAT WE DISCOVER IS CORRUPTED AND MIS-USED.
WE HAVE NO POWER.
THESE GAUNTLETS. THEY ARE POWER. POWER THAT BELONGS IN THE HANDS OF THOSE THAT DESERVE IT.
POWER IS NOT TO BE GIVEN AWAY.
POWER IS TO BE USED. THE GAUNTLETS... THEY CRY OUT TO BE USED.
WITH THEM, I CAN FORM ANY WEAPON I WANT. THEY TELL ME THE PERFECT ONE TO USE IN ANY GIVEN SITUATION.
ALL I HAVE TO DO IS TRUST THEM.

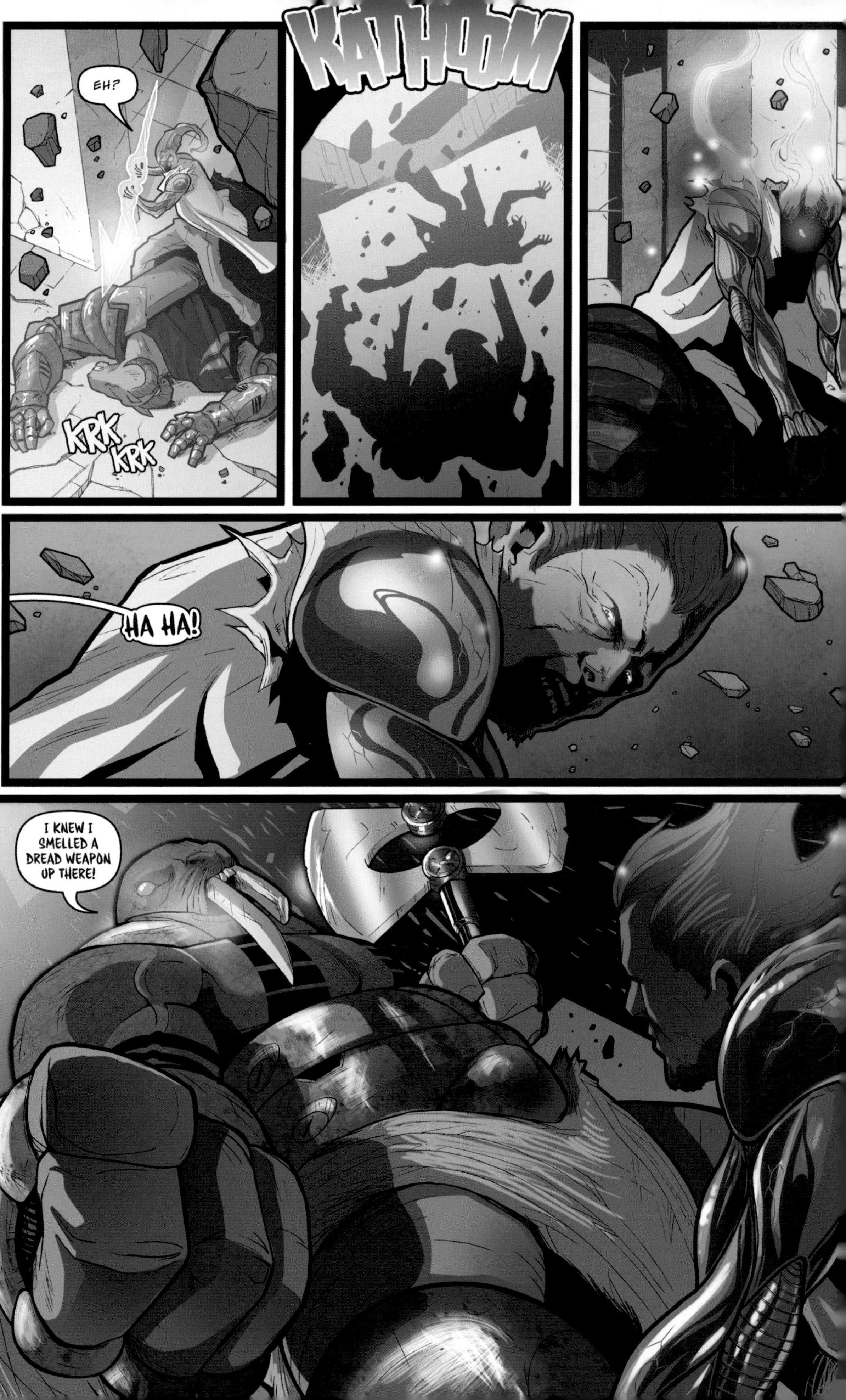
EH?
KRK KRK
KATHOOM
HA HA!
I KNEW I SMELLED A DREAD WEAPON UP THERE!

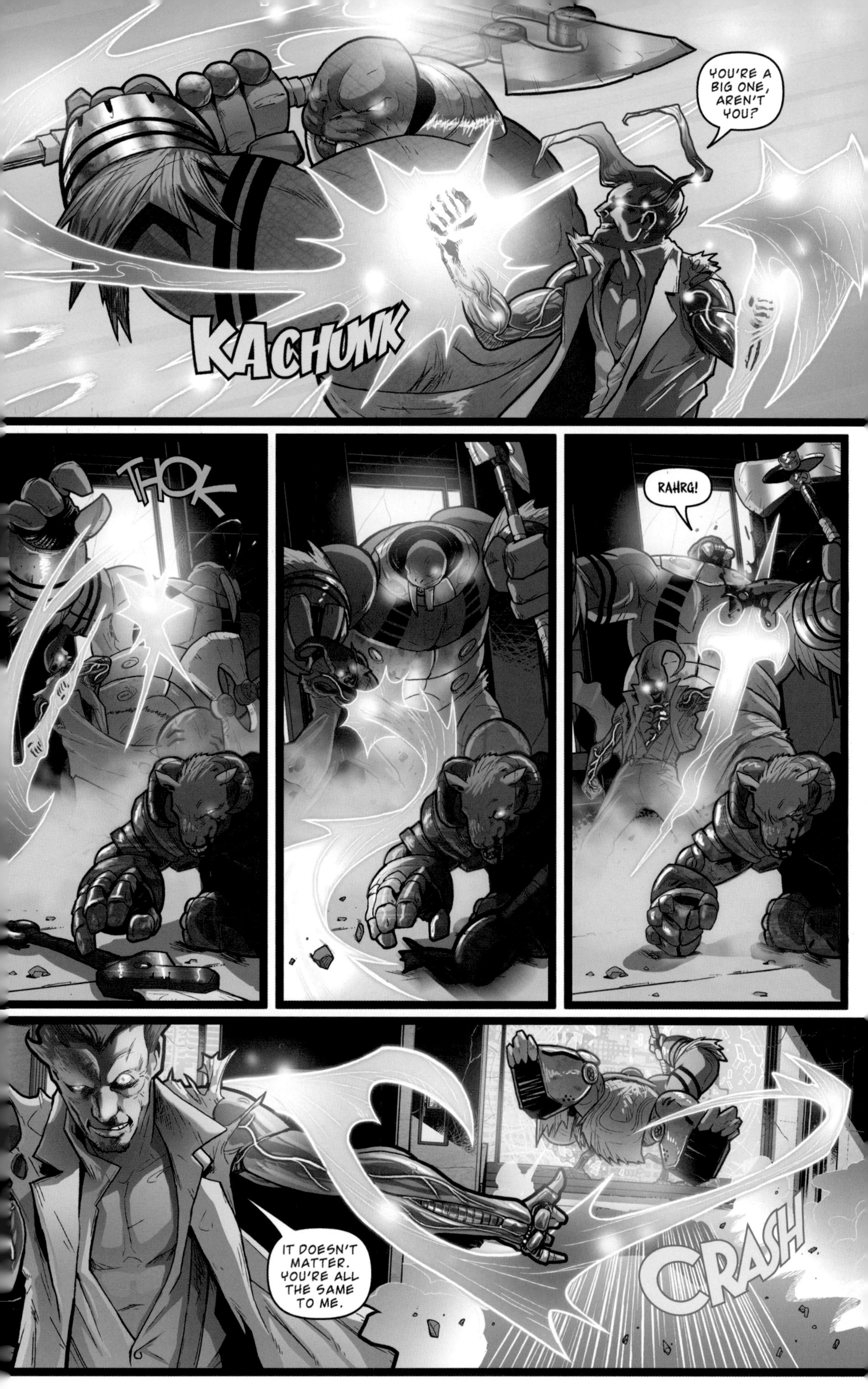
YOU'RE A BIG ONE, AREN'T YOU?
KACHUNK
THOK
RAHRG!
IT DOESN'T MATTER. YOU'RE ALL THE SAME TO ME.
CRASH

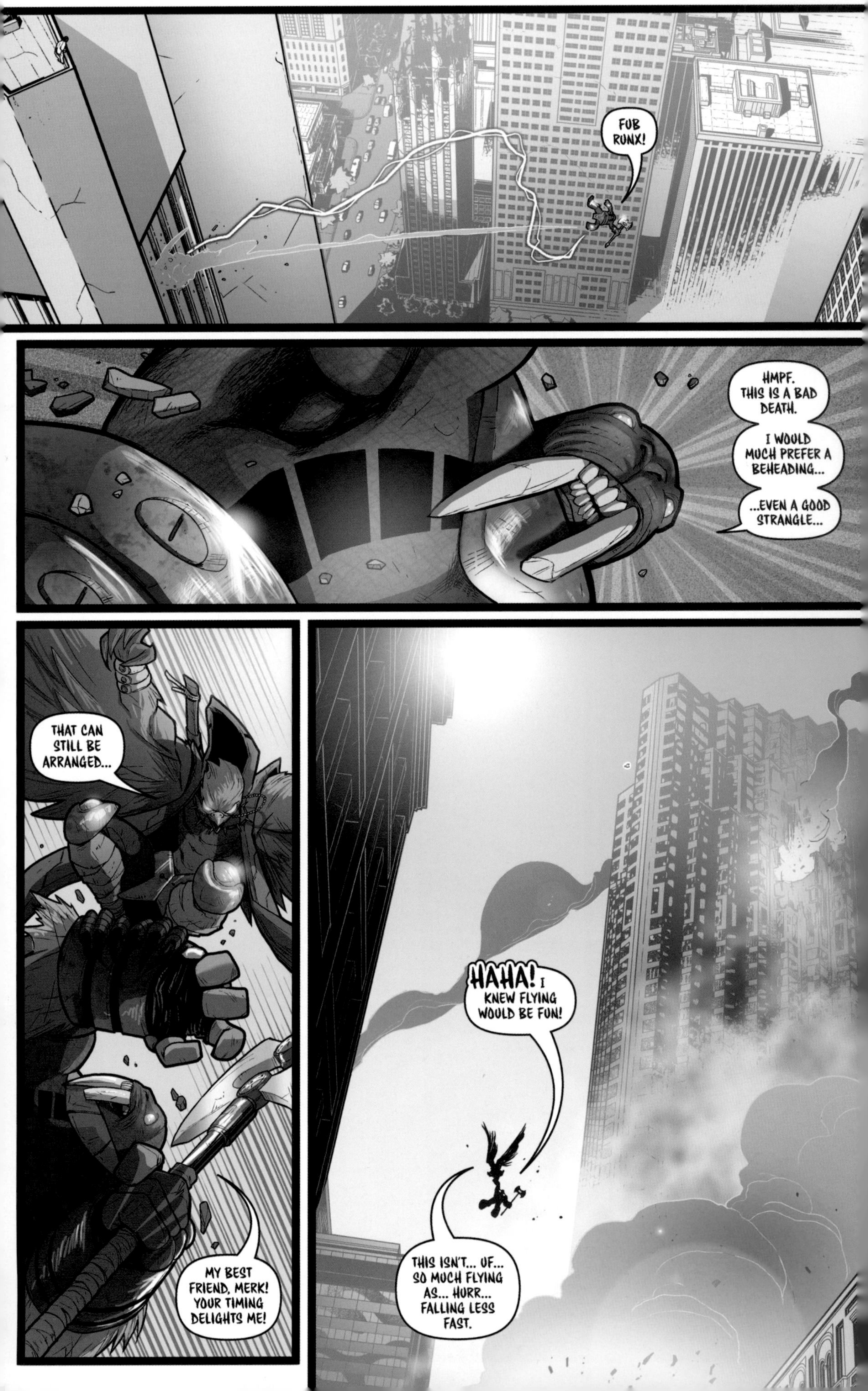
FUB RUNX!
HMPF. THIS IS A BAD DEATH.
I WOULD MUCH PREFER A BEHEADING...
...EVEN A GOOD STRANGLE...
THAT CAN STILL BE ARRANGED...
MY BEST FRIEND, MERK! YOUR TIMING DELIGHTS ME!
HAHA! I KNEW FLYING WOULD BE FUN!
THIS ISN'T... UF... SO MUCH FLYING AS... HURR... FALLING LESS FAST.

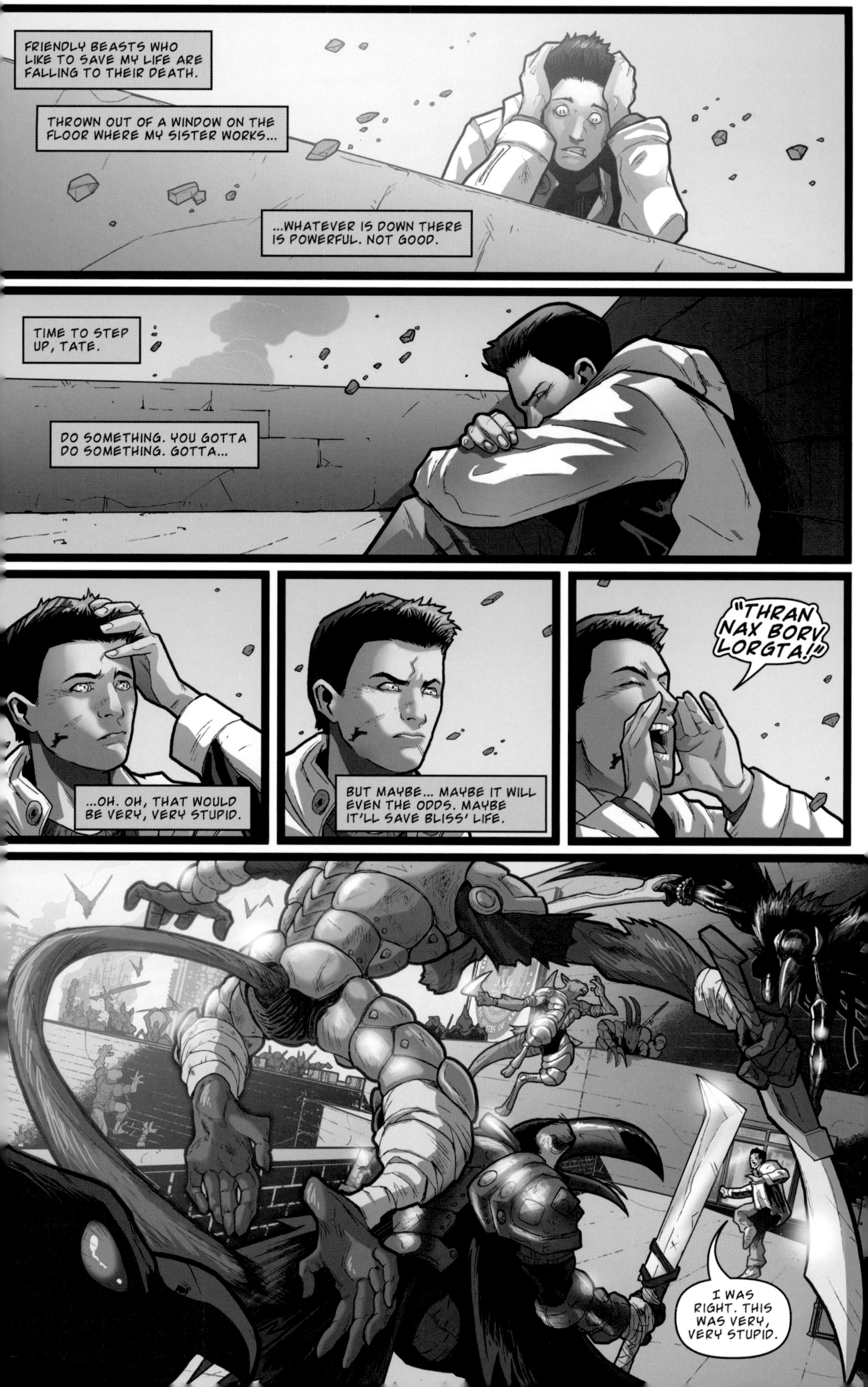
FRIENDLY BEASTS WHO LIKE TO SAVE MY LIFE ARE FALLING TO THEIR DEATH.
THROWN OUT OF A WINDOW ON THE FLOOR WHERE MY SISTER WORKS...
...WHATEVER IS DOWN THERE IS POWERFUL. NOT GOOD.
TIME TO STEP UP, TATE.
DO SOMETHING. YOU GOTTA DO SOMETHING. GOTTA...
...OH. OH, THAT WOULD BE VERY, VERY STUPID.
BUT MAYBE... MAYBE IT WILL EVEN THE ODDS. MAYBE IT'LL SAVE BLISS' LIFE.
"THRAN NAX BORV LORGTA!"
I WAS RIGHT. THIS WAS VERY, VERY STUPID.

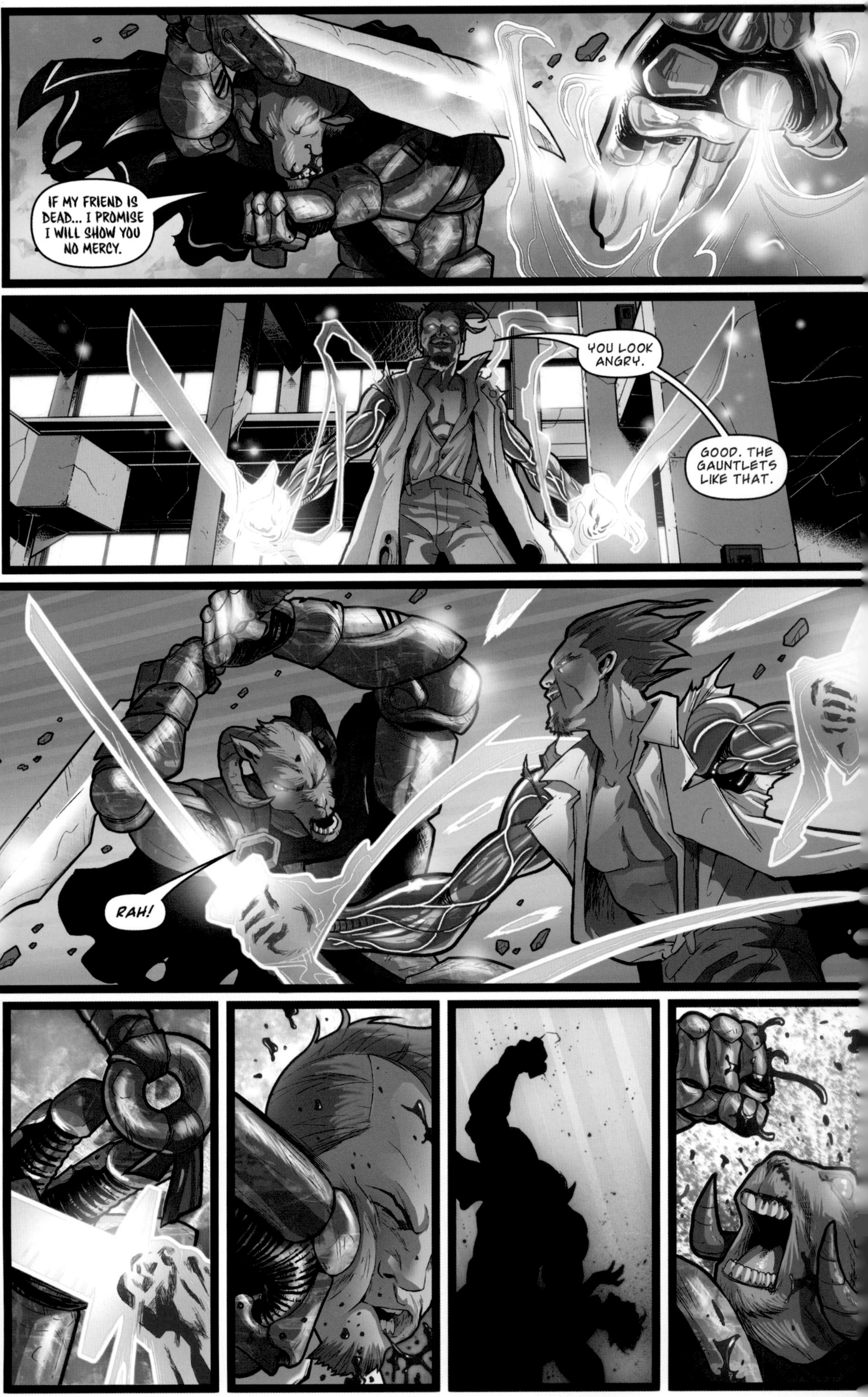
IF MY FRIEND IS DEAD... I PROMISE I WILL SHOW YOU NO MERCY.
YOU LOOK ANGRY.
GOOD. THE GAUNTLETS LIKE THAT.
RAH!

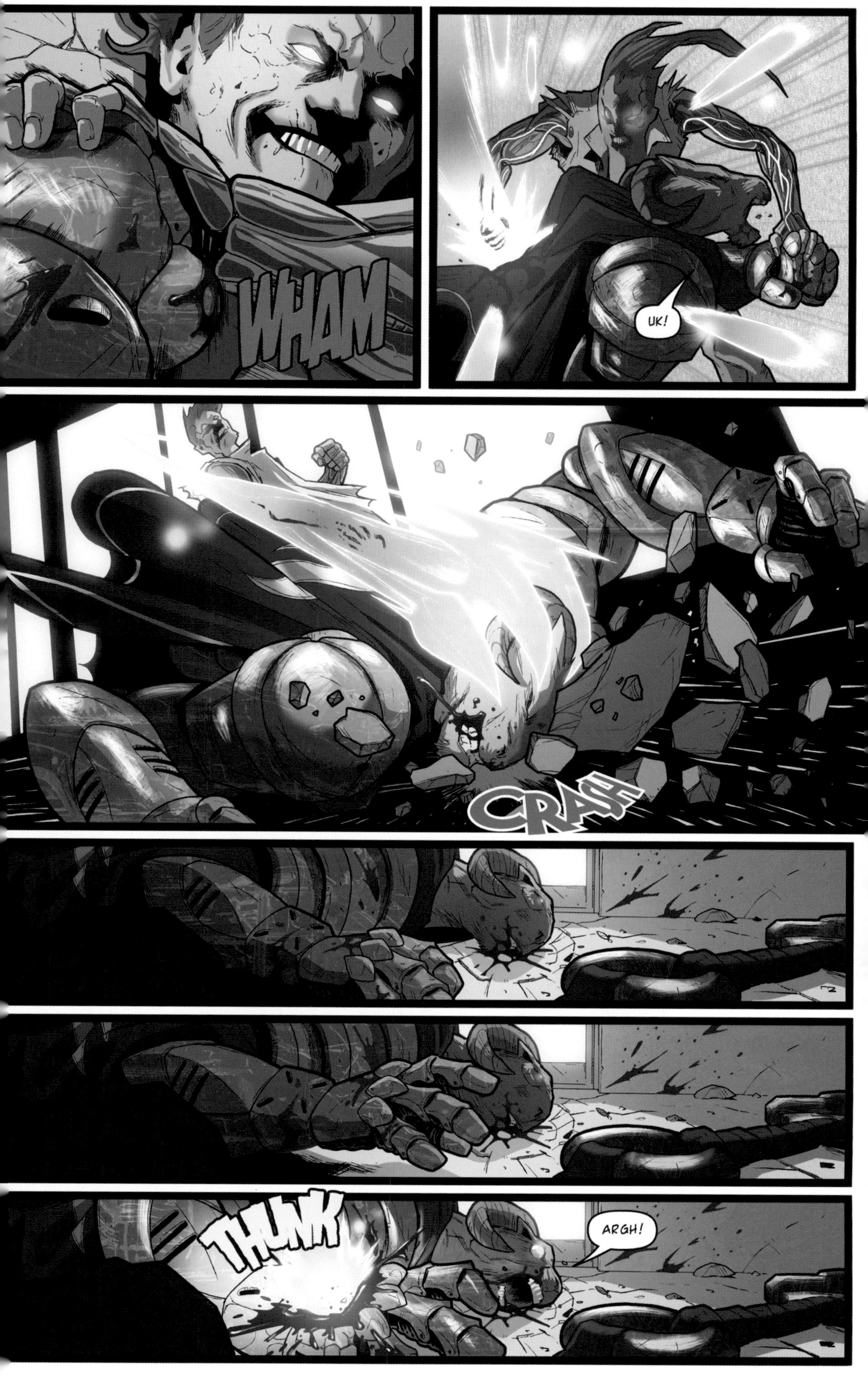
WHAM
UK!
CRASH
THUNK
ARGH!

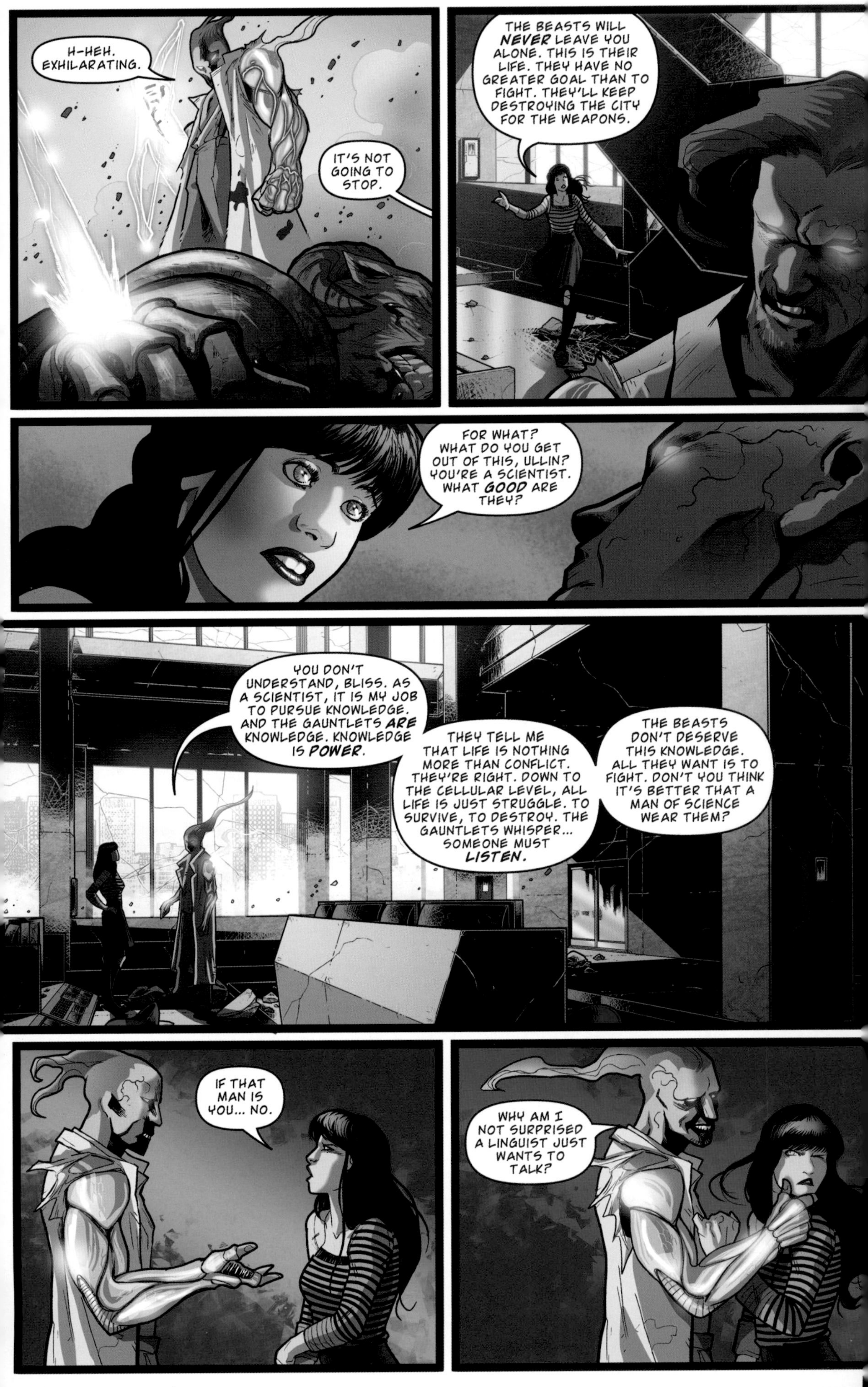
H-HEH. EXHILARATING.
IT'S NOT GOING TO STOP.
THE BEASTS WILL NEVER LEAVE YOU ALONE. THIS IS THEIR LIFE. THEY HAVE NO GREATER GOAL THAN TO FIGHT. THEY'LL KEEP DESTROYING THE CITY FOR THE WEAPONS.
FOR WHAT? WHAT DO YOU GET OUT OF THIS, ULLIN? YOU'RE A SCIENTIST. WHAT GOOD ARE THEY?
YOU DON'T UNDERSTAND, BLISS. AS A SCIENTIST, IT IS MY JOB TO PURSUE KNOWLEDGE. AND THE GAUNTLETS ARE KNOWLEDGE. KNOWLEDGE IS POWER.
THEY TELL ME THAT LIFE IS NOTHING MORE THAN CONFLICT. THEY'RE RIGHT. DOWN TO THE CELLULAR LEVEL, ALL LIFE IS JUST STRUGGLE. TO SURVIVE, TO DESTROY. THE GAUNTLETS WHISPER... SOMEONE MUST LISTEN.
THE BEASTS DON'T DESERVE THIS KNOWLEDGE. ALL THEY WANT IS TO FIGHT. DON'T YOU THINK IT'S BETTER THAT A MAN OF SCIENCE WEAR THEM?
IF THAT MAN IS YOU... NO.
WHY AM I NOT SURPRISED A LINGUIST JUST WANTS TO TALK?

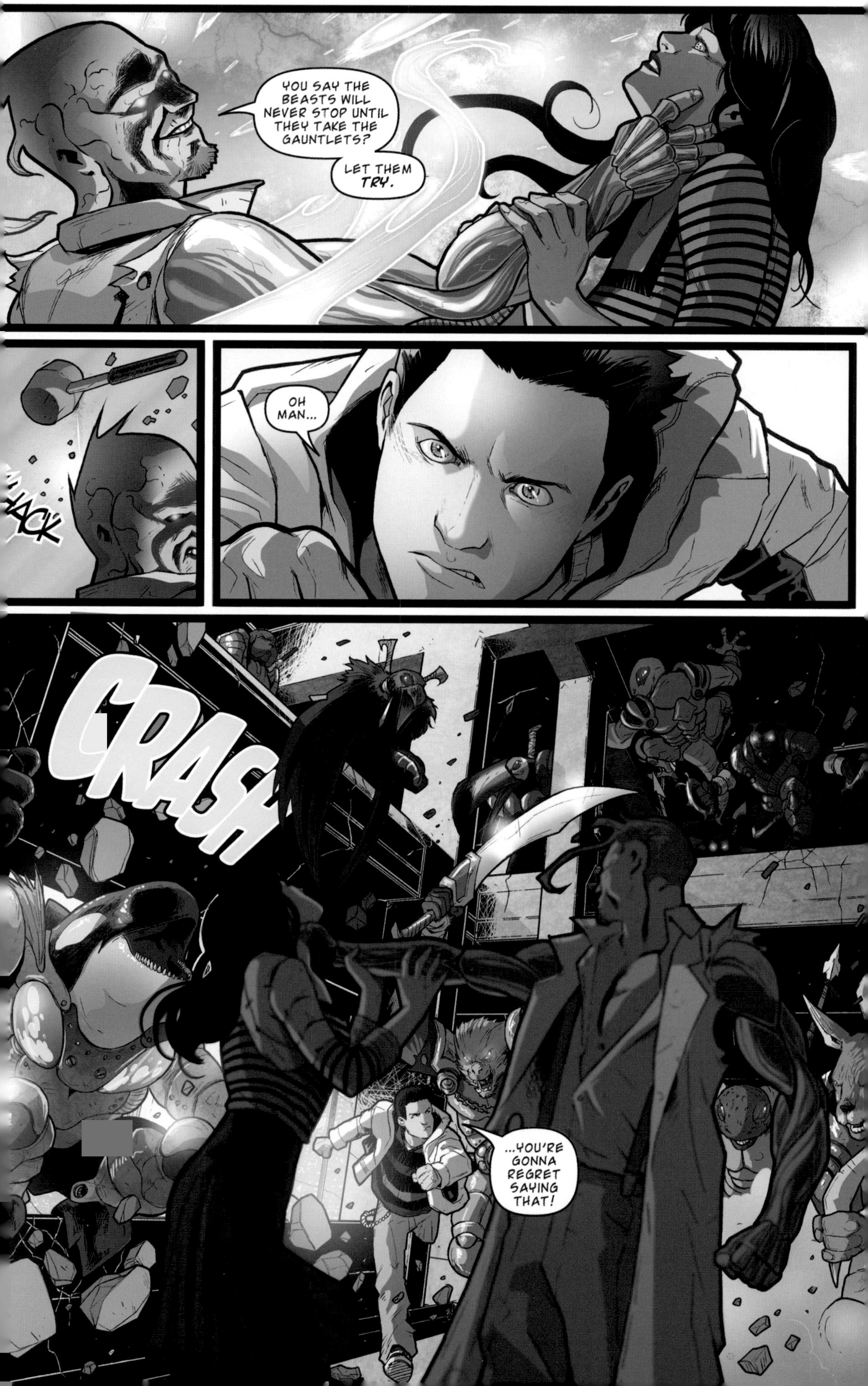
YOU SAY THE BEASTS WILL NEVER STOP UNTIL THEY TAKE THE GAUNTLETS?
LET THEM *TRY*.
OH MAN...
CRASH
...YOU'RE GONNA REGRET SAYING THAT!

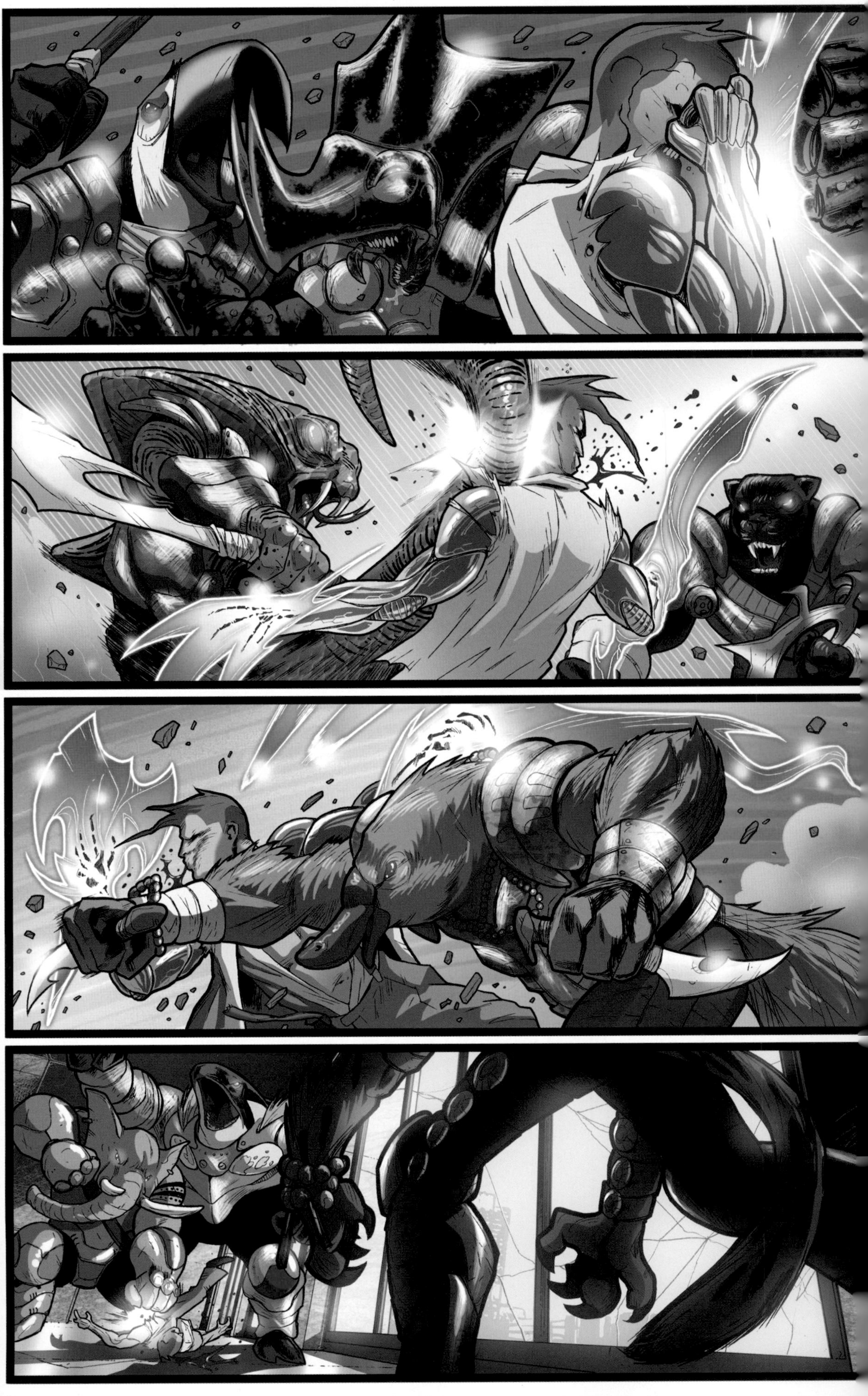

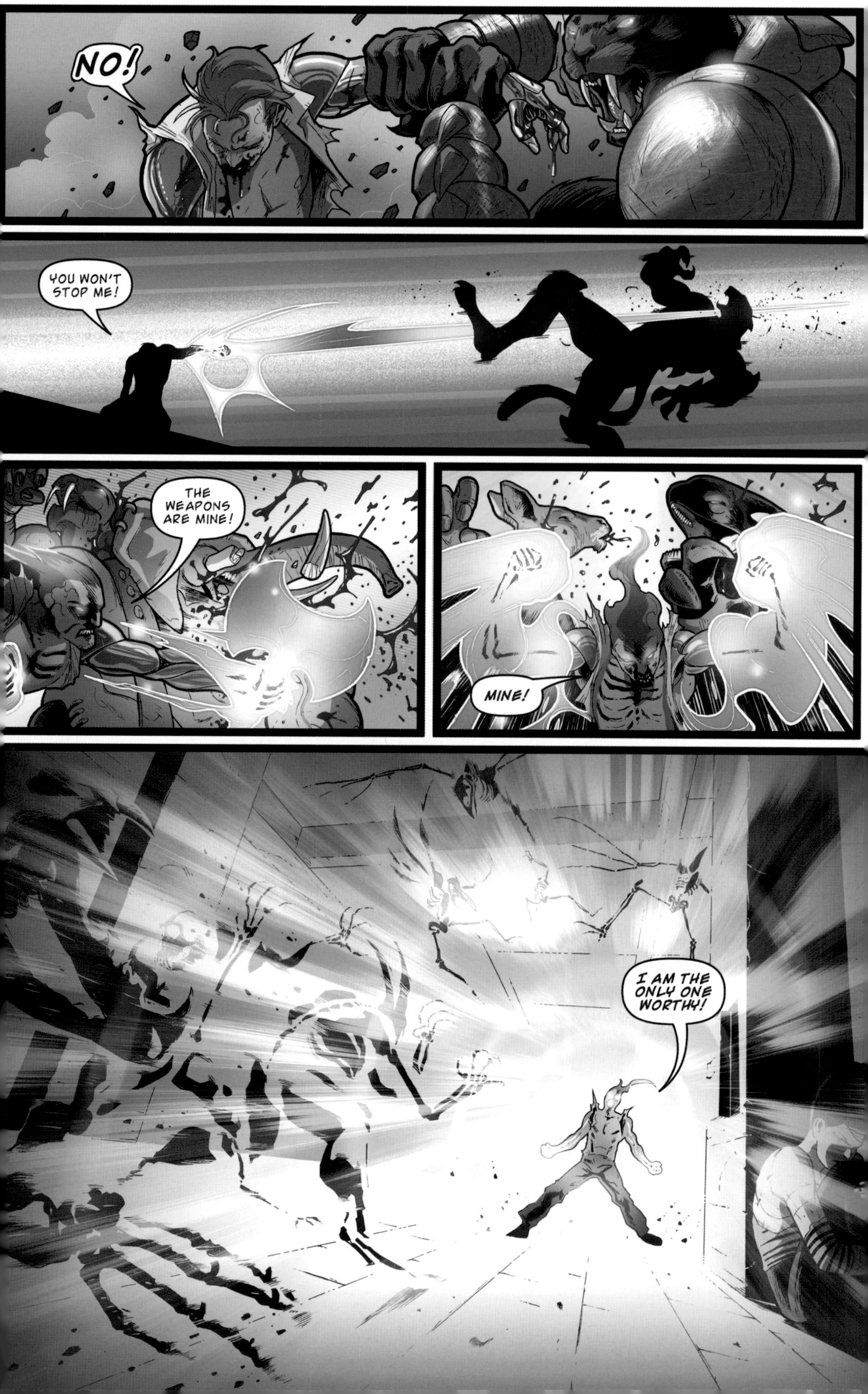
NO!
YOU WON'T STOP ME!
THE WEAPONS ARE MINE!
MINE!
I AM THE ONLY ONE WORTHY!

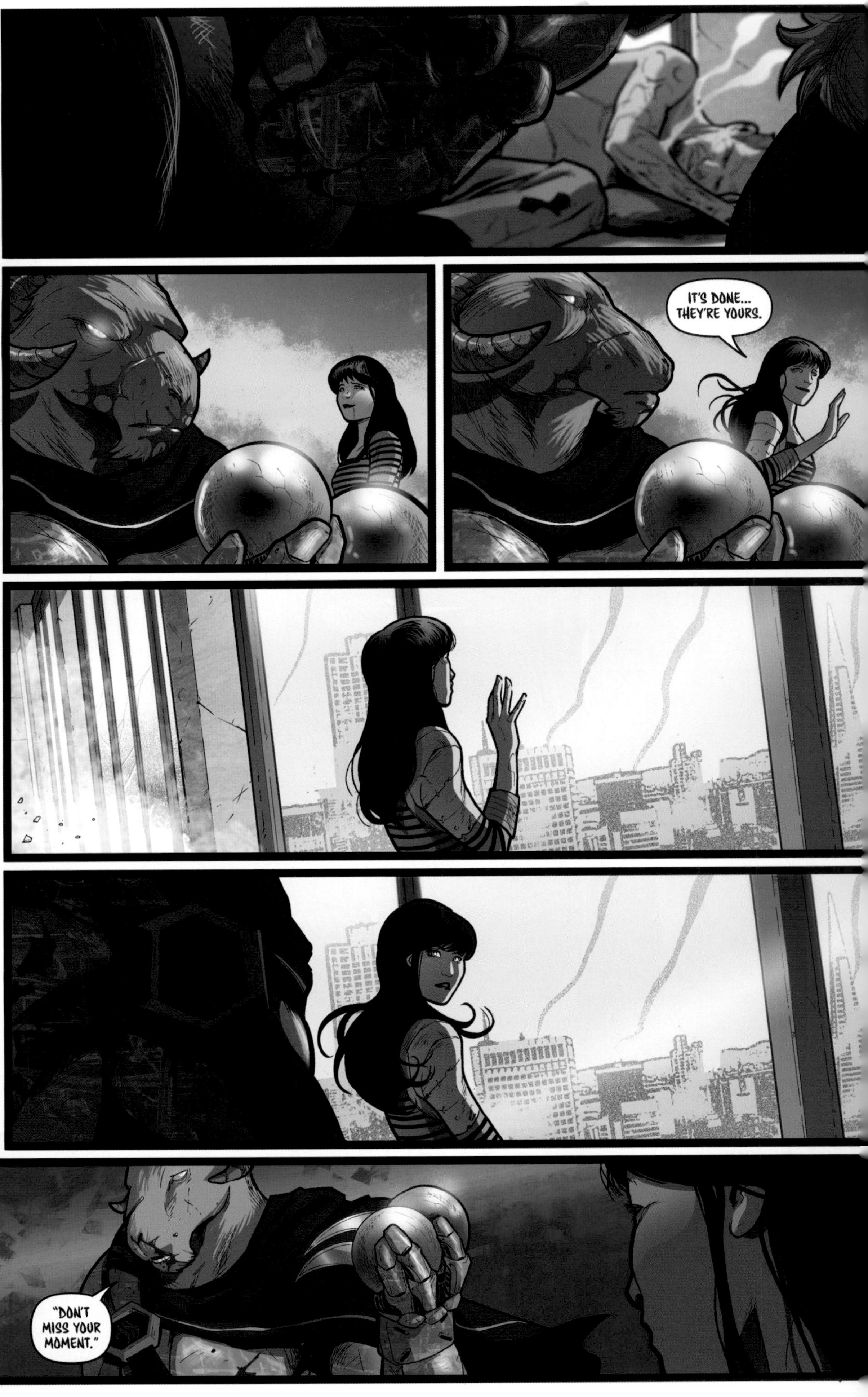
IT'S DONE... THEY'RE YOURS.
"DON'T MISS YOUR MOMENT."

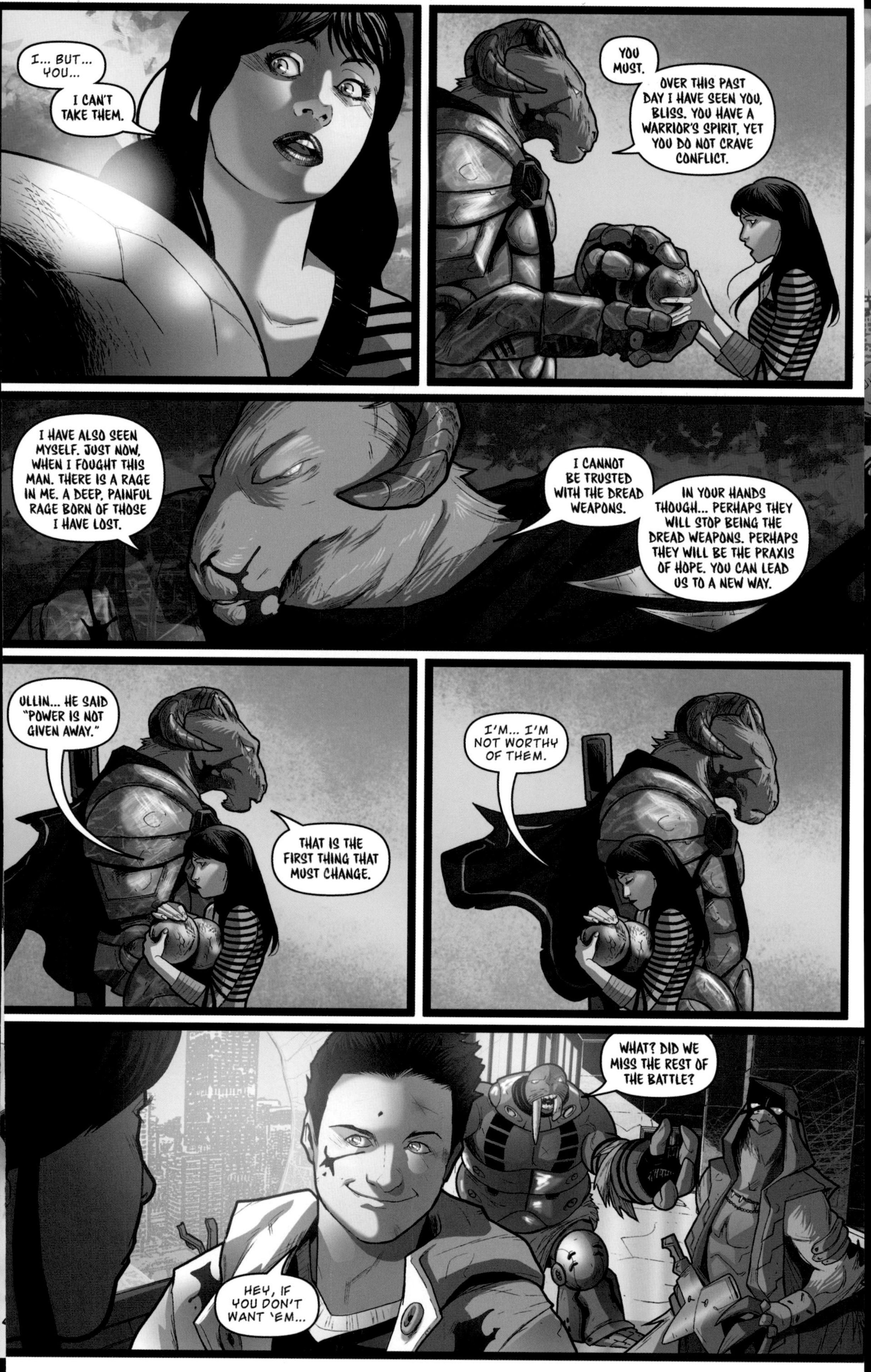
I... BUT... YOU...
I CAN'T TAKE THEM.
YOU MUST.
OVER THIS PAST DAY I HAVE SEEN YOU, BLISS. YOU HAVE A WARRIOR'S SPIRIT, YET YOU DO NOT CRAVE CONFLICT.
I HAVE ALSO SEEN MYSELF. JUST NOW, WHEN I FOUGHT THIS MAN. THERE IS A RAGE IN ME. A DEEP, PAINFUL RAGE BORN OF THOSE I HAVE LOST.
I CANNOT BE TRUSTED WITH THE DREAD WEAPONS.
IN YOUR HANDS THOUGH... PERHAPS THEY WILL STOP BEING THE DREAD WEAPONS. PERHAPS THEY WILL BE THE PRAXIS OF HOPE. YOU CAN LEAD US TO A NEW WAY.
ULLIN... HE SAID "POWER IS NOT GIVEN AWAY."
THAT IS THE FIRST THING THAT MUST CHANGE.
I'M... I'M NOT WORTHY OF THEM.
WHAT? DID WE MISS THE REST OF THE BATTLE?
HEY, IF YOU DON'T WANT 'EM...

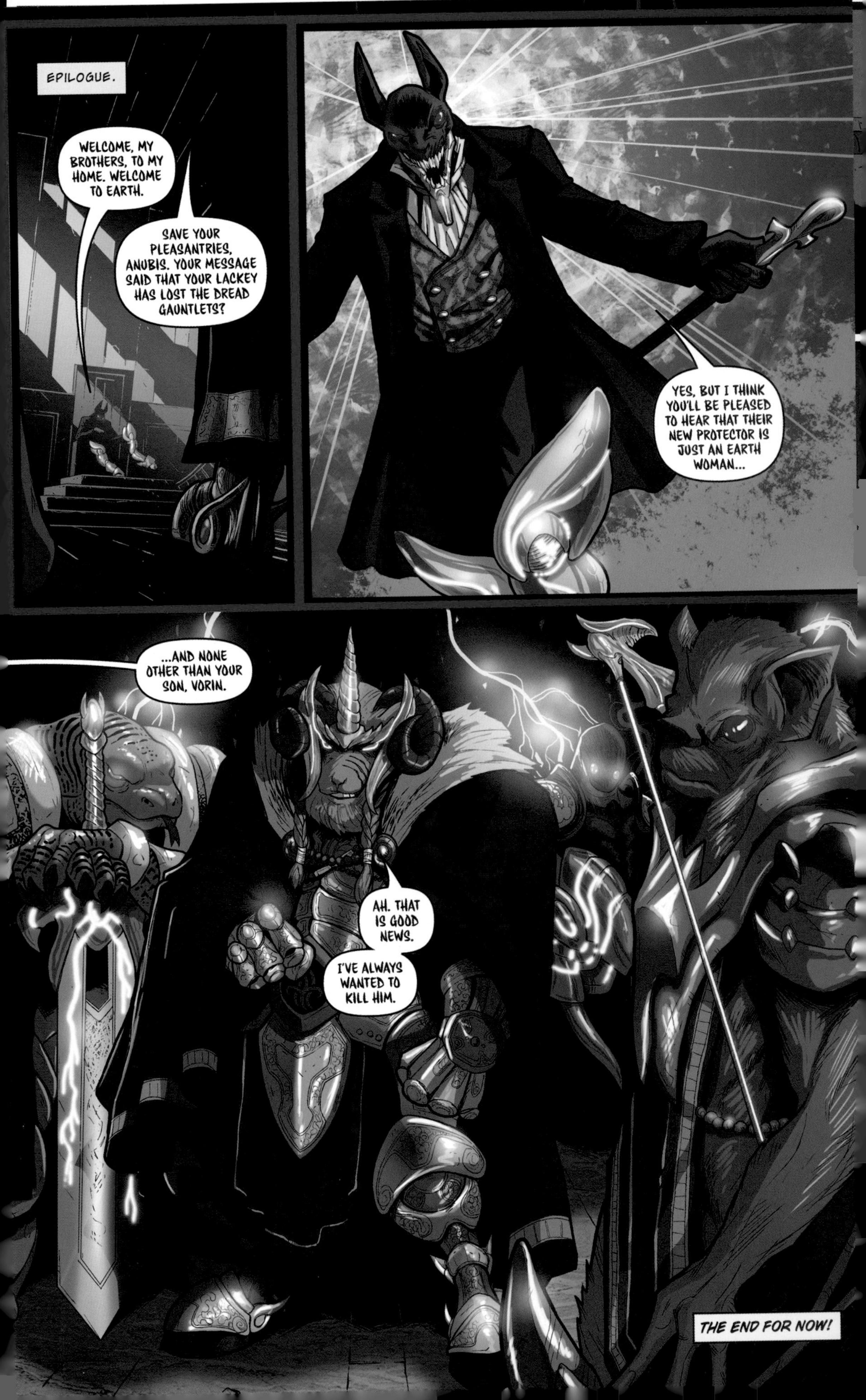
EPILOGUE.
WELCOME, MY BROTHERS, TO MY HOME. WELCOME TO EARTH.
SAVE YOUR PLEASANTRIES, ANUBIS. YOUR MESSAGE SAID THAT YOUR LACKEY HAS LOST THE DREAD GAUNTLETS?
YES, BUT I THINK YOU'LL BE PLEASED TO HEAR THAT THEIR NEW PROTECTOR IS JUST AN EARTH WOMAN...
...AND NONE OTHER THAN YOUR SON, VORIN.
AH. THAT IS GOOD NEWS.
I'VE ALWAYS WANTED TO KILL HIM.
THE END FOR NOW!

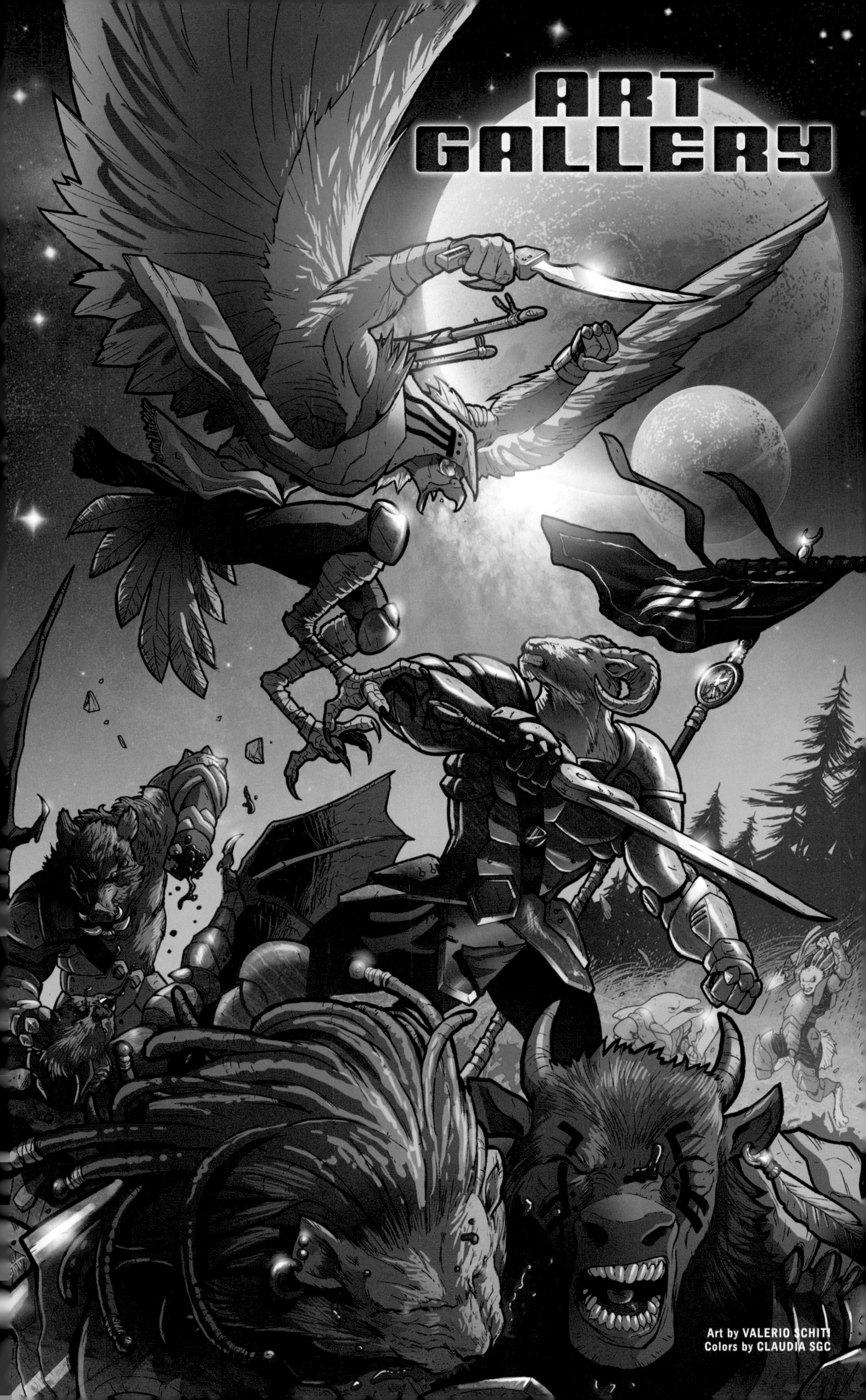
ART GALLERY
Art by VALERIO SCHITI
Colors by CLAUDIA SGC

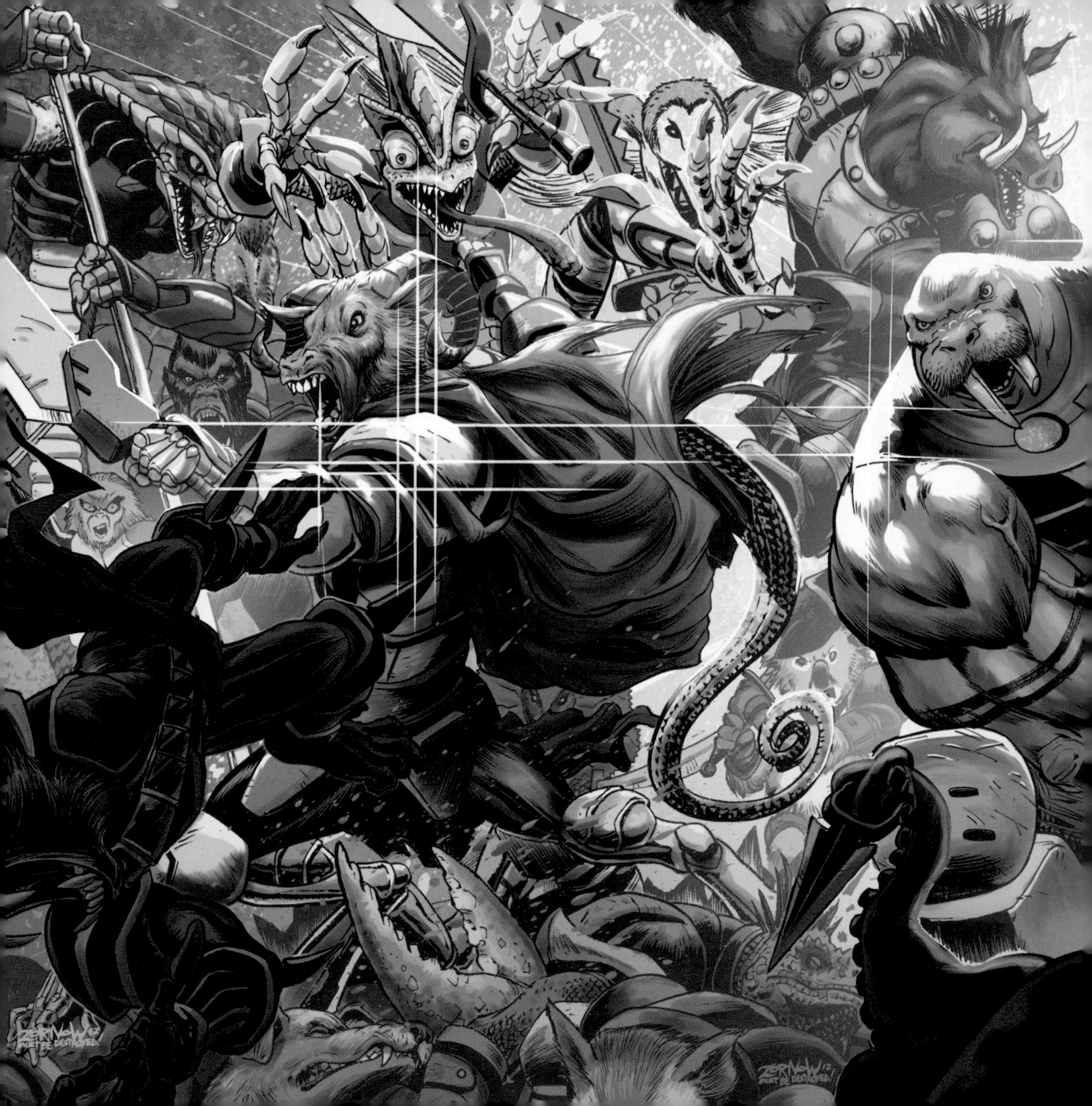

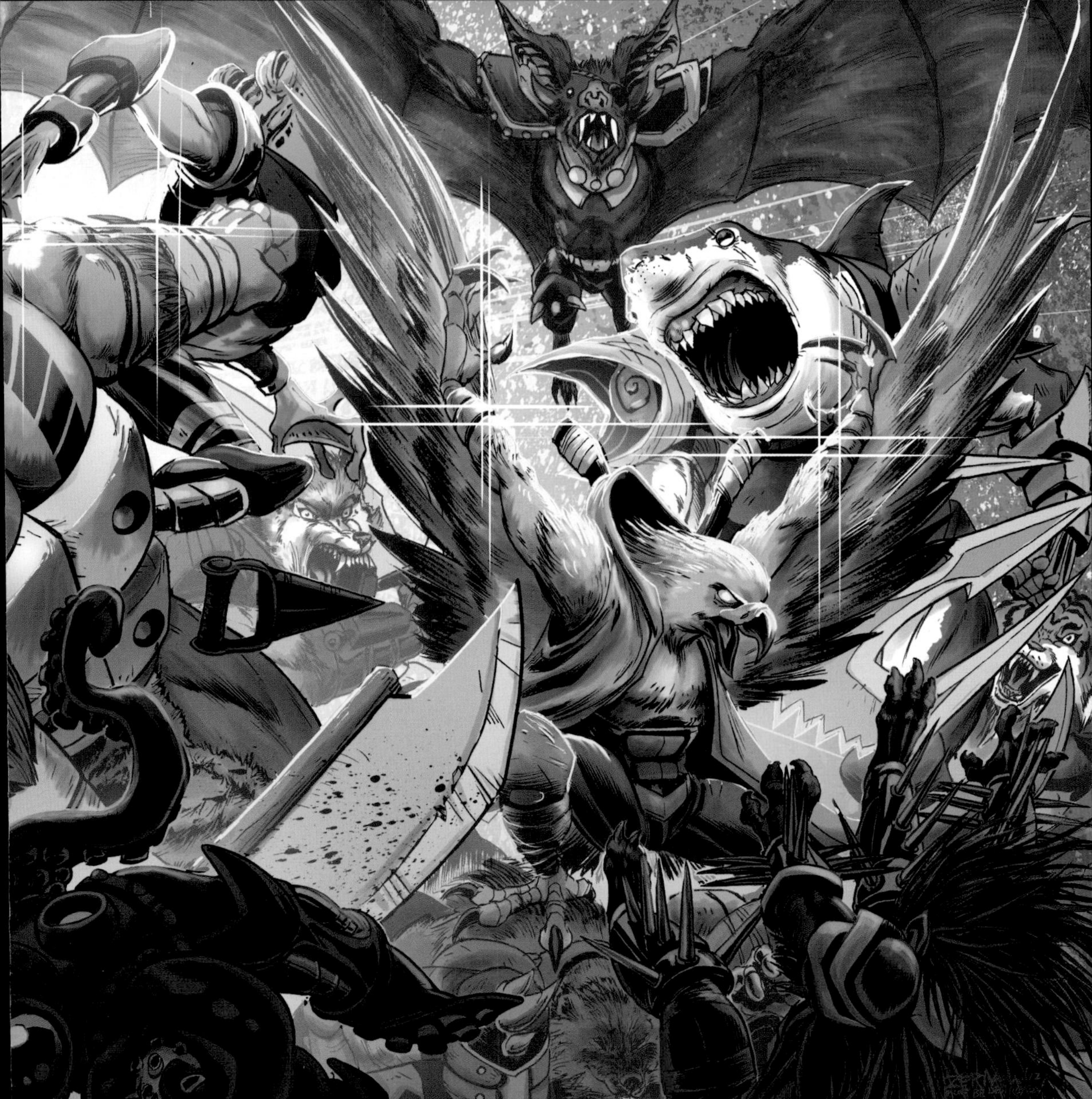

Art by JEFF ZORNOW

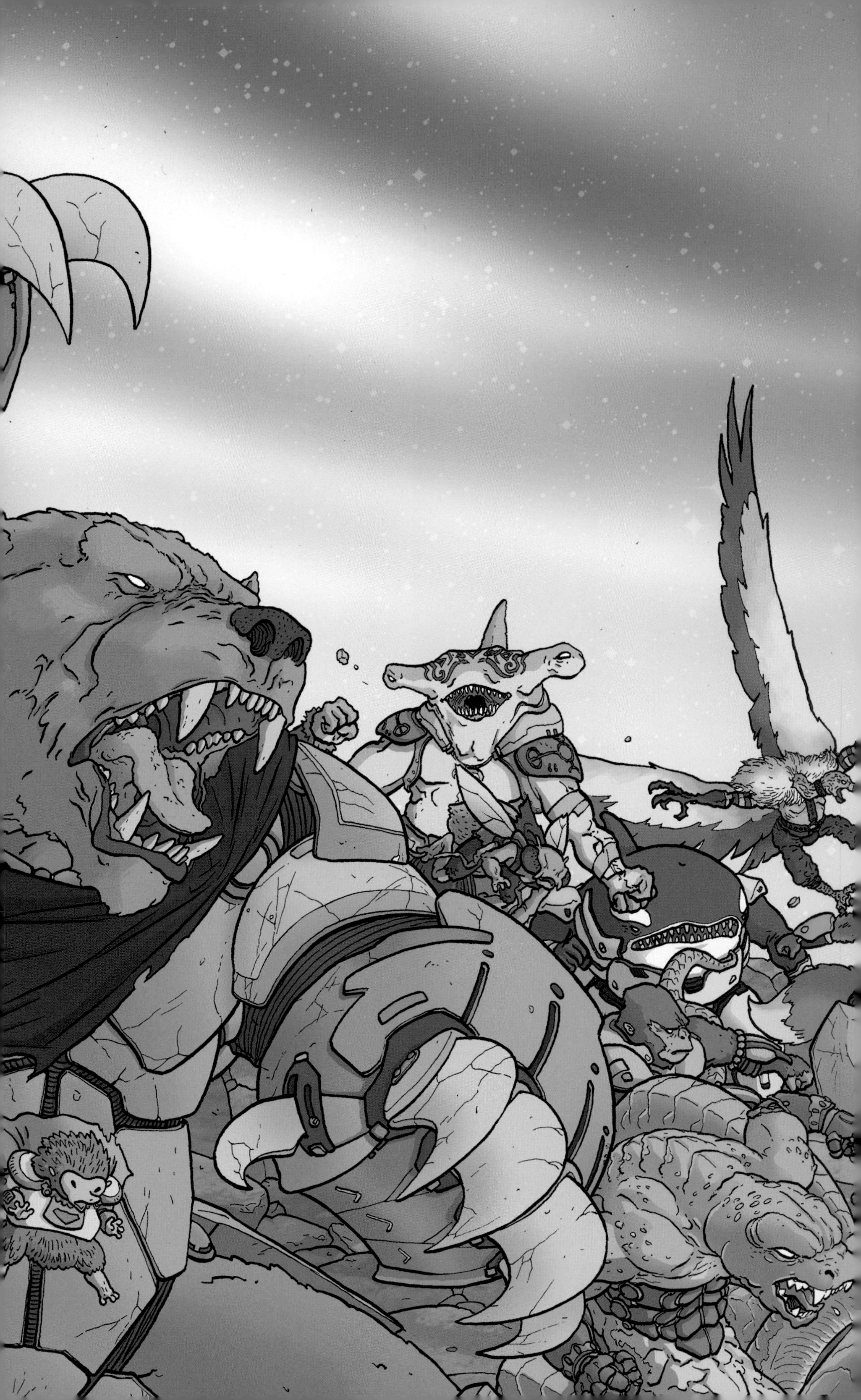

Art by **ULISES FARINAS**

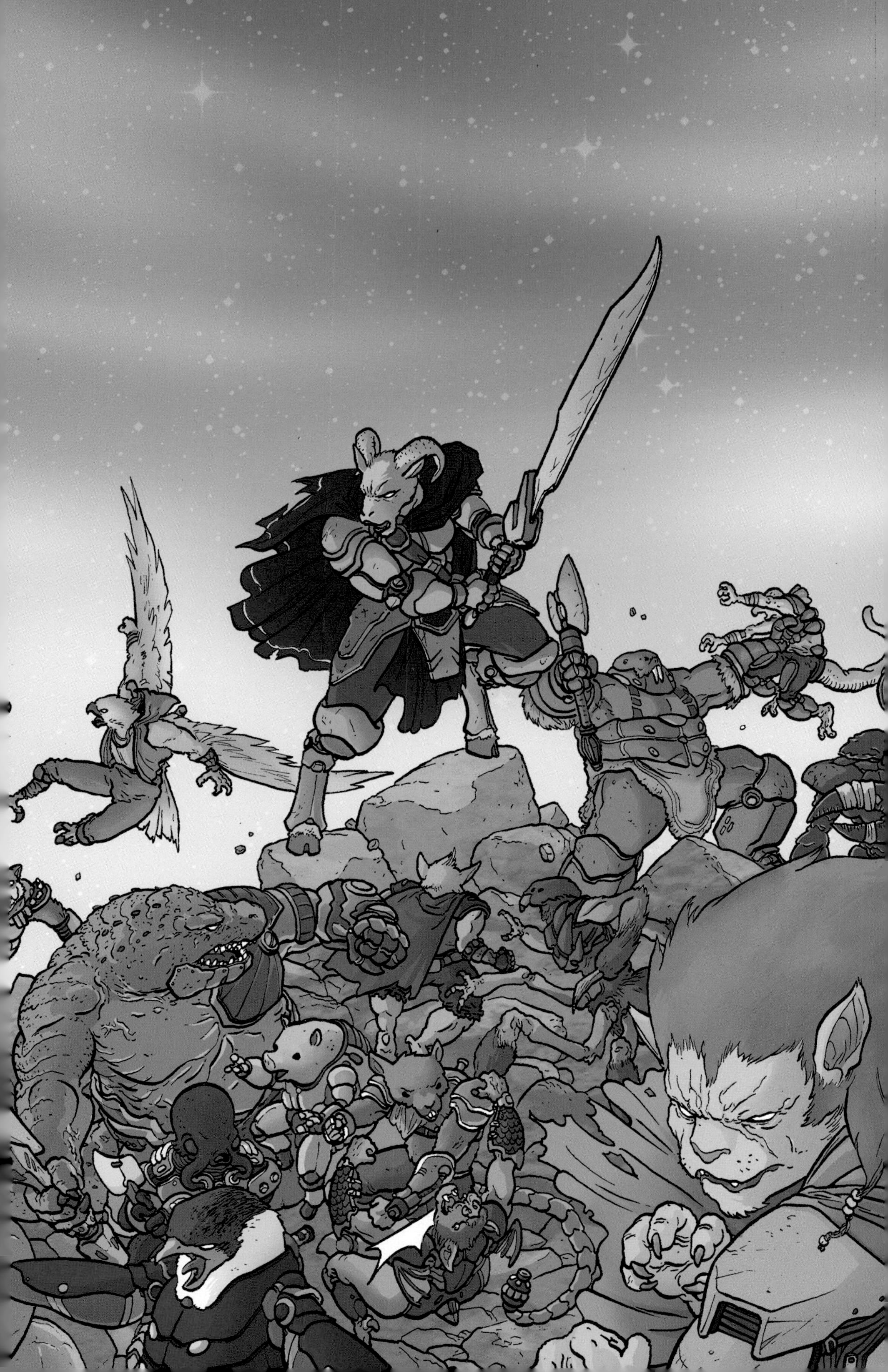

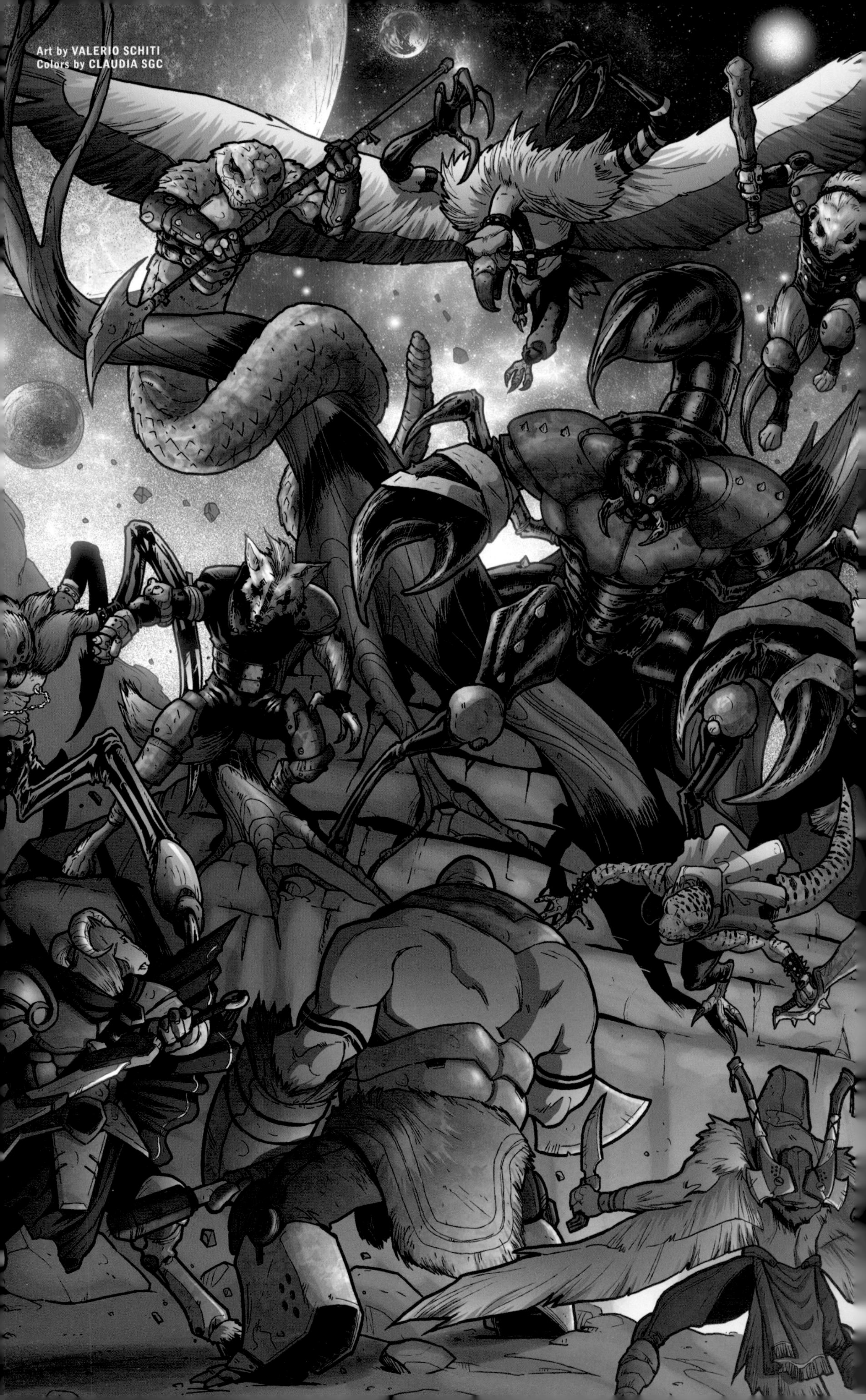
Art by VALERIO SCHITI
Colors by CLAUDIA SGC